RENEWALS 458-4574
DATE DUE

WITHDRAWN
UTSA Libraries

THE AMERICAN in SAUDI ARABIA

by Eve Lee

intercultural press inc.

Published by Intercultural Press, Inc.
70 W. Hubbard Street
Chicago, IL 60610

Copyright © 1980
Intercultural Press, Inc.

Joint Copyright © October 1977
Saudi Arabian Airlines, Kansas City, Missouri
Center for Research and Education, Denver, Colorado

First Edition October 1977
Second Edition July 1978
Third Edition November, 1980

Library of Congress Catalogue Number 80-83093
ISBN 0-933662-11-4

This publication may not be reproduced, stored in a retrieval system, or transmitted in whole or in part, in any form or by any means electronic, mechanical, photocopying, recording or otherwise without prior written permission.

Printed in the United States of America

THE AMERICAN IN SAUDI ARABIA
TABLE OF CONTENTS

	Page
Preface	v
Introduction	vii
1. Who Are You? A Cultural View	1
2. The American in America	3
3. The Saudi in Saudi Arabia	8
4. The American in Saudi Arabia	20
Situation 1 Who's Rude to Whom?	21
2 Getting Down to Business	23
3 One Saudi is a Crowd	25
4 Of Skimpy Skirts and Other Dress	27
5 Brown-Bagging It On Fast Days	29
6 To Admire or Not to Admire	31
7 Letting Them Know What You Think	33
8 The Shutter Bug	35
9 Goldbrick or Devotee	37
10 God and Man in Saudi Arabia	39
11 Smugglers' Due	41
12 Alcohol And Ambiguity	43
13 The Inevitable Cup of Coffee	45
14 What Kind of Men *Are* These?	47
15 What's Wrong with Billy?	49
16 Beware of Assumptions	51
17 Entertaining Saudi Guests	53
18 What Happens in a Saudi Home?	55
19 Abigail's Anxieties	59
20 Terry's Tribulations	62
5. Culture Shock and the Adjustment of Lifestyles	65
6. Enjoying Yourself in Saudi Arabia	75
7. Saudi Arabia: Some Basic Facts	89
Resources	106

LIBRARY
The University of Texas
At San Antonio

PREFACE

Many Americans who have lived in Saudi Arabia, and many of the Saudis who worked with them, have contributed to this book by sharing their experiences with us. Some spoke with nostalgia, some reflected the frustrations inherent in cross-cultural relations, others still glowed from excitement. All agreed that most people going to Saudi Arabia need to know much more than they do about the country and about how to cope with the differences they will encounter. Each was enthusiastic about THE AMERICAN IN SAUDI ARABIA and its approach to examining the significant cultural differences between Saudi and American people and how to deal with their differences.

The book itself is the work of a number of hands. An earlier version has been used for several years by Saudia Airlines in training their American employees. Saudia personnel have provided valuable feedback for use in this revision. Special appreciation goes to the publishers of THE GREEN BOOK: GUIDE FOR LIVING IN SAUDI ARABIA, published by Middle East Editorial Associates (see bibliography) for permission to use their research data. We are indebted as well to two other excellent books: UPDATE: SAUDI ARABIA, published by the Intercultural Press and Assignment: SAUDI ARABIA, published by Bechtel Corporation. David Hoopes of the Intercultural Press, Inc., Nessa Lowenthal of Bechtel Corporation, Kathy Sullivan of AMIDEAST and Stephen Hanchey of International Training Associates provided direct assistance in revising and critiquing the manuscript and suggesting resources for its improvement. The excellent photographs are the work of John B. Nichol, a cross-cultural consultant who recently returned from the Kingdom.

Whether you have already arrived in Saudi Arabia or are preparing to go, and whether you are experiencing euphoria or anticipation anxieties, we hope you will stop and ponder carefully the information presented and the questions raised in this book.

Eve Lee
October, 1980

vi / THE AMERICAN IN SAUDI ARABIA

Photograph by John B. Nichol

INTRODUCTION

It is no simple matter to live in another country. Those people who do, discover that there is a conflict between their own inclination to do things the way they always have and the expectations of their hosts that things be done *their* way. Many people who move to foreign countries don't have the faintest idea what to do about this conflict.

It may have to do in part with the concept of what is "foreign." In our country, America, that which is foreign is what is different from that which is American. We speak of "foreign countries" or "foreign cultures." The problem is that when we travel to these "foreign" countries a reversal takes place and it is *we* who are foreign rather than they.

This fact seems obvious when written down as it is here. But when a person, or a family, goes abroad the obviousness disappears—for two reasons. First, there is so much to do just to get established in a new location that there remains little time or energy to appreciate the subtleties of what is "foreign" and what is not. Second, whenever we go abroad we carry with us not only baggage containing our possessions but our "cultural" baggage as well. This cultural baggage consists of ways of looking at things, ways of thinking, ways of behaving and ways of communicating which are not only peculiar to our own country and culture but are so much a part of us that we assume they are normal or universal to *all* human beings. It often comes as a shock to discover profound differences in the most simple life processes and to find ourselves asserting the foreignness of our hosts when we are the ones who are foreign.

As one person put it:

> The important thing to remember is that people living in another country aren't defective Americans. Their customs may be very different from ours, but that doesn't make them wrong. Their ways are right for them, and they won't change them for us. Why should they?
>
> After all, we're the foreigners in their country. We should adjust to them. Americans certainly don't change their ways to accommodate foreigners coming to the United States. We expect them to adjust to us.

A little strongly phrased, but essentially true.

The principal problem, however, and the problem we are addressing in this book, is that the personal disruption which often occurs within individuals as a result of a clash of cultures can be so debilitating that it prevents them from being effective in their jobs, limits the ability of families to adjust to the new environment and may end in "failure" and an early return home.

There are various estimates of the number of Americans who "fail" in overseas assignments, ranging anywhere from 15% to 40%. (These are only the obvious failures. Many more are the hidden failures, the people who perform marginally even though they stay on the job.) The price of such failures is high, anywhere from fifty to several hundred thousand dollars for an employee and family who must be replaced—usually not because of inadequate technical skills, but because they could not cope with the cultural differences. Even the marginal failures may cause untold damage either in dollars, ill will, or both, through blunders of ignorance or insensitivity.

Finally, it is important to remember that those serving in assignments abroad are functioning on a world stage in which their personal and organizational interests are strongly linked to the interests of their country. To be provincial, insensitive, arrogant or paternalistic, to show disrespect for other cultures, or to display an overweening belief in the superiority of one's own culture is to do a disservice to oneself, to one's employer and to one's country. It can also deprive one of most, if not all, of the real pleasure that may be derived from exploring and learning other ways of living.

Which brings us to Saudi Arabia. Many people believe that Saudi Arabia and the U.S. share a special relationship based on oil, development and the mutual desire to maintain stability in the Middle East. This relationship links us to a country with deeply rooted customs and traditions but one which is rapidly being transformed from an ancient nomadic society into a modern industrial state. The language, the traditions, and the climate are radically different from what most Americans are used to. At the same time, the new and up-to-date may be seen everywhere, often in dramatic and confusing juxtaposition with the old. Sorting out these aspects of contemporary Saudi Arabia and coming to terms with the reality of the culture is not easy for most Americans, but it can be as rewarding as it is challenging for the open-minded visitor.

It is the purpose of this book to help people who are going to Saudi Arabia understand that the Saudi way is as normal and "right" for the Saudis as the American way is for Americans and to aid them in developing the ability to cope effectively with and, indeed, to enjoy the differences they encounter.

Technical information on the logistics of relocation, getting travel documents, finding housing and schools, locating needed services, etc., will not be included in this book (though we will make reference to sources of such information). Our concern instead will be with the differences in culture and lifestyle Americans will encounter in Saudi Arabia and with the ways in which the conflicts and dislocations arising out of that encounter may be dealt with most effectively.

1

Who Are You?
A Cultural View

To the question, who am I?, you might answer: I am a man or I am a woman. Or you might identify yourself by occupation: I am a mechanic or a businessman or an engineer. You might choose religion: Mormon, Catholic, Methodist; or ethnic group: Black, Chicano, Italian. You might feel you are, most importantly, a parent or a homemaker. Or you might say: I am an American.

It is your identity as an American that is most important here—because when you go to Saudi Arabia, at least in the beginning, you will be seen principally as an American rather than the more unique individual you perceive yourself to be. Being an American you will also be seen as a bearer of American "culture." While it may be argued that there are strong regional and ethnic differences in the U.S., there are nevertheless certain underlying cultural patterns, ways of seeing and doing things, that are shared by the vast majority of people in this country.

One of the most important things for you to do, then, as an American going to Saudi Arabia, is to become more aware of your own culture.

But what, you may ask at this point, *is* this vague generality called "culture"?

In Western society, we often speak of a "cultured person," by which we usually mean someone who appreciates, understands and is able to discuss the arts, classical music, literature, the theater and the like. Is this what is meant by "culture"?

In the U.S., we have a whole series of activities throughout the year that are labeled "cultural events." They range from opera and art exhibits to rodeos, baseball games and the numerous ethnic celebrations which take place across the country. Is that what is meant by "culture"?

Well, yes and no. These are *manifestations* of culture, that's true. But "culture," as we are using the term here, is not what we *know,* nor is it a collection of social activities. Culture consists of the deep and complex ways of thinking and behaving that emerge from the totality of the experience a group of people have shared over time. It is expressed not only in art and social events, but in values and religious beliefs and in such everyday behaviors as keeping appointments, getting married, signing documents, making love, greeting people, rearing children, even dying. We begin learning our culture from the moment we are born so that what it tells us to do and the way it wants us to think become habitual and unconscious.

Individually we may disagree with some of what society proclaims as culturally acceptable attitudes and behaviors, but culture is still the dominant force in shaping our assumptions about life and the values, attitudes and behaviors which result from them.

Your ability to recognize cultural influences in your own attitudes and actions is important in developing "cultural awareness" so that when you encounter differences in Saudis, differences which may seem strange or even unpleasant, you will be able to recognize them as cultural differences rather than as some kind of violation of a universally correct way of behaving.

2

The American In America

What are Americans like? Or, as a visitor asked: what is American about Americans?

Think about that question for a moment. Then jot down some of the basic characteristics, attitudes, values, ways of behaving or living which you think are most typical of us or which you think might make us stand out in Saudi Arabia.

Here's our list:

Americans are *informal*.

They live at a *fast pace*.

They are *direct* in conversation and social relations.

They believe in *equality*.

They prefer to live in *nuclear families*.

They believe they can exercise *control over nature*.

Let's explore each of these in a little more detail.

Informality

We're a diligently casual people. Friendliness and openness are primary virtues. We deny the importance of rank and are uncomfortable at formal occasions and in formal clothes—at least most of us are. We like to call people by their first names as soon as we meet them and we are not averse to asking relatively personal questions of a relative stranger. We like to establish relationships quickly.

Does this informal behavior indicate a lack of respect? Some people think so. But to us, respect and informality are not related. Using first names rather easily is taken as a sign of acceptance and friendliness, not rudeness.

- Our aversion to recognizing social rank is such that many of us make a point of resisting any special deference to age or position. We will defer to achievement but little else.
- A casual "Hi" or "So long" often take the place of more formal greetings or leave-taking which involve embraces or hand-shakes. But again, rudeness is not intended.
- Such questions as "Where do you work?" "Do you have any children?" "Do you play golf?" "What is your score?" are not meant to be personal or prying. It's just a way of telescoping longer processes of establishing acquaintanceships. It enables people to find common interests on which to base a conversation and to get to know each other. We're a mobile population in a large country. We must be able to establish friendships quickly before we move on to a new place.

But to many people we come on too fast and too strong. Our barrage of questions seems to be an invasion of privacy for those who keep their private and public lives distinct and separate.

- We also pay a price for the easy making and breaking of friendships; they tend to lack the depth which characterize relationships in less mobile societies.

Living at a Fast Pace

To us "time is of the essence." Time is unquestionably one of the most valuable and important commodities in American life. Americans seem to be able to waste everything but time. "Time is money." Placing this importance on time—on saving it, on using it, on not wasting it—leads to a hectic pace and the appearance of ignoring some of the amenities of living and of social relationships on which many cultures place great stress.

- We eat fast foods and hurry to appointments. We expect people to be "on time," and "to get right down to business." We place great value on achievement, which means using our time productively.

- We tend to live our lives by the clock. We're impatient with delays and often seem brusque, if not rude. We tend, in fact, to forgive the brusque person because "his time is valuable, too."

Directness We like a person who is frank, open and direct. We consider forthrightness and outspokenness to be virtues, signs of honesty and integrity.
- We like to "face facts," "go straight to the source," "meet the problem head on," "put our cards on the table," "get the unvarnished truth," and "tell it like it is."
- We can take criticism, if it isn't too personal, without being offended. We also like to challenge authority, to question, to analyze and probe. The intention, however, is to seek answers rather than to criticize or challenge the individual as a person.

There are others whose sense of interpersonal relations is quite different from ours, to whom frankness is simply rude. Indeed in many cultures it is more important to tell people what they want to hear, rather than hurt them with the truth. It is a matter of courtesy and is not considered dishonest.

Equality We like to think of ourselves as living in a classless society—even though there are marked class and social distinctions in the United States. But in general we are egalitarian. We believe people are created equal and should have equal opportunity.
- Even though classes exist, it is relatively easy for Americans to move from one class to another. Position is earned more often through personal merit than family identification or some other indication of status.
- Americans are practical and like to tinker. We take pride in doing things ourselves and are not averse to manual labor, no matter what our social role is.

- Paradoxically, no matter how friendly and egalitarian we believe we are, we often treat laborers and serving people (bellhops, waiters, taxi drivers, maids, shopkeepers, etc.) very impersonally, almost as if they were invisible.

Families

We tend to live intense, intertwined lives in small families: mother, father, the immediate children—the so-called nuclear family. In a large country like ours with a high degree of mobility, families spread out, linkages with grandparents, aunts, uncles, cousins are stretched and weakened.

- Consider for a moment the degree to which we divorce, live singly, lose contact with "distant" relatives. In many parts of the world, the family—extended to include distant aunts, uncles and cousins—is so encompassing that everyone has obligations to everyone else, virtually as if they were brother and sister, or parent and child.
- Our families often function as units. All ages eat together, even when company is present, and do things together regularly. Men and women, children and adults do not live significantly segregated lives. Women, while still fighting what they feel to be sexist traditions, are comparatively independent and unrestricted. This "liberation" is not universal and is rare indeed in Saudi Arabia.
- We value our family relationships, but family connections do not play a large role in the structure of the society. Children like to be independent and parents are often embarrassed when seeking special privileges or opportunities for their offspring.

Control Over Nature

American culture embodies in a high degree the basic Western assumption that humans are superior to and have the right and responsibility to strive for a mastery over nature in whatever way will benefit them. Even though in recent years this assumption has been severely questioned—as we recognize our capacity to exhaust or destroy nature's life-supporting capabilities—it nevertheless governs many fundamental American attitudes.

- Americans reject fatalism. We believe that we as much as any other force—natural or supernatural—have the ability to affect the course of our own lives. What is "achieved" by our own efforts is thus a subject of admiration.
- We are also problem-solvers. We reduce experience to "problems" and then use our technological and other skills to solve them. What results is "progress". Progressive improvement of self and society are things to which we are almost universally, and sometimes obsessively, committed.

Stop now and look back over the values embodied in the characteristically American attitudes we have described here.

Imagine a society with the opposite, or sharply contrasting, values.

How would you feel suddenly dropped into a country and culture which varied radically from your own in so many critically different ways?

3

The Saudi In Saudi Arabia

To say that Saudi Arabia is a land of contrasts sounds trite, like the introduction to a travelogue. But nowhere in the world is this more true, not so much because of differences in the natural environment—though these are great—but because modern technology has struck the country with tremendous force and brought about changes that are dizzying in their visual impact. These changes, which in other countries have been spread over several generations, are occurring in Saudi Arabia in a few short years. Diesel trucks and jet airplanes are replacing camel caravans, though the camel has not yet been discarded. Modern architecture and broad, tree-lined avenues are replacing mudbrick houses on twisting streets, although mudbrick buildings are still evident. The nomadic Bedouins still move in groups from place to place, but it is now common to see a pickup truck or a big sedan parked beside the traditional tent.

You may be surprised by its modern look, especially in the larger cities. Oil wealth is rapidly changing the face of Saudi Arabia, and the traditional lifestyle is being affected by the impact of Western technology. However the country remains conservative and tends to be faithful to its orthodox interpretation of Islam and true to its cultural heritage. The tradition of centuries still lies near the surface of Saudi life.

It is therefore important for the newcomer to know something about its pretechnical natural environment, about its history and cultural traditions, about the Royal House of Al-Saud, and about other aspects of Saudi society as they were before the onset of modernization.

Particularly important is knowledge of the religion. There is no separation of church and state here. Islam not only controls the personal lifestyle of the people but their system of government as well. Religion pervades Saudi life.

What do you know about Islam? For most Americans it is probably a jumble of images; mosques and minarets, men in flowing robes riding great Arabian steeds and brandishing crescent-shaped swords, masses of people kneeling in prayer, prayers chanted incomprehensibly and monotonously, Mecca.

But what is Islam in Saudi Arabia really like?

Religion

The impact of Islam on the culture and society of the Middle East, and particularly on the Kingdom of Saudi Arabia, cannot be overstated. More than a once-a-week religion, it permeates all of life, based on the five pillars of the faith, affecting Muslim and non-Muslim alike. Islam has, therefore, a strong influence on Saudis attitudes, feelings and behaviors.

- Five duties are prescribed for all Muslims. These are outlined below. Each duty is described in the Koran and has been amplified and refined by legally appointed religious scholars through the ages. These duties are widely and often strictly observed in the Kingdom.

The most pervasive and most subtle effect of Islam, however, is in the reliance of the people on it as a sustaining force. This is expressed in the frequently heard terms, "Inshallah" (God willing) and "Alhamd'allah" (thanks God).

There is a firm belief that everything that happens is God's will and man cannot alter the course of events that He sets. Hardship is endured with equanimity, good fortune comes as a blessing from God, and it is assumed that what happens in life is the will of God. For anyone staying in Saudi Arabia for any length of time, the encounter with Islam will be constant, not only as adjustments are made to the observations of Islam but in dealing with the underlying manifestations of the beliefs that are part of it.

- The constitution and legal system are based directly on Islamic law, called the *Shariah*. It tells the believer how to live righteously and the community at large how to conduct its affairs, spiritual and temporal. Modernization and the use of technological systems have, in recent times, required new bodies of government regulations to deal with conditions created by these changes. In addition, many of the old teachings are being interpreted more liberally in line with the requirements of modernization. The orthodox ties remain important, however, and in situations of conflict between religious and secular considerations of principle, those of religion take preference.

The Five Pillars of Faith

Profession of faith: This consists of repeating the basic creed: "I submit that there is no god but God and Muhammad is His prophet." (Muslims recognize Noah, Abraham, Moses and Jesus as prophets sent by Allah to the people prior to Muhammad, although Muhammad is considered the "last and greatest prophet." According to Islam, Christians, Jews and Muslims all worship the same God.)

Prayer: Five times a day—at dawn, midday, in the latter part of the afternoon, at sunset, and in the evening—a Muslim turns toward the Kaabah (Holy Place in Mecca) to pray. These prayers, which are detailed, ritual performances, are ordinarily a private affair which may be performed singly or in groups wherever Muslims chance to be at the appointed hours. But on Friday (the weekly day of rest) congregational prayers are held in the mosques at midday, and all men are expected to be present.

Alms-giving: The Koran stipulates that all believers must give to the needy. Formerly an obligatory tax (zakah) paid to the government for this purpose, alms-giving is now a personal act and ranges from 2% to 10% or more of one's yearly income.

Fasting: Throughout the month of Ramadan, an observant Muslim abstains from food and drink (as well as practicing continence in other respects) from dawn to sunset. A cannon is fired as a signal for the beginning and end of each day's fast.

Pilgrimage to Mecca (Hajj): This is set apart from the other four pillars of Islam because it requires a Muslim to perform this act of piety (at least once in a lifetime) only if he has the means and is physically able. A Muslim of the purest faith may live and die without ever having been able to go to Mecca. But the merit is great for one who goes and performs all the rites and ceremonies prescribed.

Ramadan

Ramadan, is the ninth month of the Islamic calendar. The first four days of the succeeding month (Shawwal) are holidays for celebrating 'Id al-Fitr, The Feast of the Breaking of the Fast. Many special delicacies are prepared at this time, and exchanging of gifts is usual.

The Hajj

The *Hajj* takes place during the twelfth month (Dhu al-Hijjah). This is the time when pilgrims from all points of the Muslim world assemble in Mecca by the hundreds of thousands.

The prescribed rituals are to be completed between the 8th and 13th days. The high point is prayer and meditation on the Plains of Arafat on the 9th day, followed by *'Id al-Adha,* the Feast of the Sacrifice, commemorating Allah's sparing Abraham the sacrifice of his son.

Hospitality

Though the Muslim saying "Honor the guest, even though he be an infidel," may grate a little on Western ears, it underlines the extreme importance of hospitality in Muslim countries. Even an enemy is assured of safety and courtesy while enjoying the status of guest. This stress on hospitality comes partly from the dependence of man upon man to survive under the harsh conditions of the desert and partly from the teachings of Islam.

- The Arab sense of hospitality originated in the early days of raiding Bedouin tribes, when food, shelter and protection from enemies were extended to all visitors. While protection is no longer a necessity, it has resulted in a degree of graciousness and courtesy to guests that makes the visit to an Arab home a memorable experience.
- All guests are served food and drink immediately. When the hospitality of a house is extended, the guest is expected to accept even though the stay is brief. At the very least on all occasions (including office visits) coffee will be offered and should never be refused.

The partaking of food and drink establishes a bond of friendship and to refuse is seen as refusing friendship.
- There are few more distasteful epithets in the Arab world than the charge of being stingy. Generosity is universally praised. A host offers as much as he can, and the best that he has. And it isn't unusual for a host to give a guest something that the guest admires.
- One of the principal Islamic duties is to give alms. "The man who has been favored with wealth must look after those who are less fortunate." Fulfillment of this duty is manifest in their concept of hospitality.

Family

All social relationships in Saudi Arabia are indirectly, if not directly, tied to family considerations.
- The family is the strongest unifying force next to Islam itself. The Arab is known by the family to which he or she belongs. Loyalty and duty to the family are greater than any other obligation—social or business.
- Defense of the family honor is one of the strongest obligations a Saudi feels, and he will go to great lengths to redress an insult to that honor. One of the reasons for the Saudi emphasis on restricting and protecting women is that the greatest disgrace that can befall a Saudi family is for one of its women to have sexual relations outside of marriage.
- The Saudi family is patriarchal. The male head rules with a firm hand. This paternalism extends to other figures of authority, such as teachers and political and religious leaders. Deference to authority and acceptance of externally imposed discipline is balanced, however, by a sense of equality that allows individuals to assert their own or their family's interest.
- The sense of family unity extends to grandparents, aunts, uncles, cousins, etc., as well as to members of the tribe. Family

members attend to each other's welfare. A man will sometimes marry the widow of a deceased brother to insure that she will be properly cared for. Younger people are expected to take care of their elders.
- Large, polygamous households (Muslim men are allowed four wives by their religion) were once the rule. The practice of taking more than one wife is largely dying out, and increasing numbers of Saudis are now living in smaller, nuclear units (man, wife and their own unmarried children). They still, however, retain extremely close ties with other members of the family.
- The family from which one comes constitutes a principal basis for being judged, favored or disfavored by others. Personal gain is considered secondary to family loyalty, and family honor is sacrosanct.

Personal and Social Relations

As with any people, Saudis have their own set of social behaviors peculiar to themselves but logical within the framework of their values. Here are some of the most significant for the American visitor to understand:
- For the Saudi the "self" is buried deep within the individual. The American self begins much nearer the surface of the body. Americans exist within what has been called an envelope of personal space which they don't like invaded, especially by strangers. Americans, for instance, don't touch in public the way the Saudis do. Since the self, that which is personal and private, is buried inside, Saudis don't consider the touching and jostling encountered in Saudi Arabian public life an invasion of privacy. It is simply a natural part of everyday existence. The whole concept of what is public and private is different in Saudi Arabia. Outside the home there is little opportunity for privacy. Even "private" business meetings may be conducted amidst a group of disinterested people.

- While the Saudi familial and social structures are paternalistic and hierarchical, there is a strain of individualism in the Saudi temperament that is immediately apparent. Saudi's tend to personalize experience and respond to it directly and emotionally as individuals or as family representatives. What results is an almost paradoxical conjunction of individuality of expression with a high degree of deference to authority.
- A Saudi cannot say "no" to a request from anyone but especially one in a position of authority or esteem. It would be impolite to do so. There are a variety of ways to deal with requests or demands that conflict with other, overriding, concerns. While showing deference for the person making the request, there will be reasons offered for delays in fulfilling it which eventually are insurmountable.
- Saudis are extremely sensitive to disparagement and to the use of strong or obscene language. Swearing or the use of obscenities degrades the speaker in the eyes of the Saudi. Mild ("Hey, you're doing that all wrong, dummy; try it this way.") or even friendly ("By golly, you're a bright son-of-a-bitch.") use of disparaging words and phrases may be seen as unforgivable insults.
- It is considered the right of every person, no matter what his position in society, to be treated publicly with visible respect and dignity.
- Experts in non-verbal communication tell us that the body speaks a language of its own and that this language varies from culture to culture. For Americans, standing close and thrusting one's face toward another is usually offensive, often an act of belligerence. For the Saudis it is an acceptable conversational style. Conversely, the use of the left hand to touch or give something to another person is quite insulting to the Saudi, but has no meaning to

the American. (In Saudi Arabia the left hand is considered "unclean" because it is the bathroom hand.) Similarly Americans often sit with their feet up on a chair, stool or desk, an act that Saudis find offensive. The feet are the most inferior part of the body to a Saudi and to show the soles of them to someone is insulting.

In general, the Saudi style of interpersonal communication is more intense than that of the American. There is a desire to be closely involved with the other person. Not only is the conversational distance less, Saudis also like direct, continuous eye contact which to an American may seem too intimate for a purely social relationship. The Saudi feels that the eyes reveal the inner being and eye contact is used to estimate the quality of the person to whom one is talking. Because of this need for eye contact, Saudis walking together carrying on a conversation will frequently stop and face each other when the discussion becomes intense.

- Touching and the olfactory sense also play an important role in Saudi communication. Where Americans, except in intimate male-female relations, prefer not to encounter the odors or body of an acquaintance, Saudis consider odors and bodily proximity important to the establishment of even a relatively casual relationship. A Saudi, during an intense conversation, will want to touch—an arm, a lapel, a hand—as this heightens the degree of communication.

The Role of Women

Arabia is a man's world. Equality of the sexes is not even an issue. Yet the role of women, like everything else in the Kingdom, is in a state of rapid change. In order to understand what is happening, you need to know something of the traditional place of women in Saudi Arabia.

- For centuries the women of Arabia lived in extreme privacy. They had separate quarters and were not seen by men other than their husbands and close male relatives. When they went outside their homes, they wore a veil and a long cloak (*abayah*) and were accompanied by a male or older female member of the household. This "seclusion" of women was viewed not as a restraint but as protection. Women were regarded as precious, and therefore in need of this protection.

- In family relations the husband's position was dominant; wives and children were obliged to submit to his authority. Divorce was the husband's prerogative. Social life was segregated by sex: men had their circle of male friends; women had their circle of female friends. (This is still true today.)
- The advent of Islam greatly enhanced the status of women, however, by limiting the number of wives a man might have, imposing restrictions on divorce, and insuring the rights of women to property and a share in the inheritance from father or husband.
- In recent years, education (even though in segregated classrooms) has been an important factor in raising the status of women. Conversation with teen-age daughters of liberal Saudi families shows that, behind their veils, young women are thinking modern thoughts and looking forward eagerly to using their education.
- Public affairs still tend to be segregated—certain times and places for the men, others for the women. But mixed social gatherings in private are becoming more common. Few Saudi women are employed in the business world, but there are an increasing number of career opportunities for women, especially in education and in certain government ministries. Saudi women continue to be veiled in public, but under many an *abayah* may be the latest in fashion from Paris or London.

- The increase in wealth and exposure to the Western world will certainly affect the family system. But it would be a mistake to assume that any really fundamental change is likely to take place. The Saudi wants the benefits of modern Western technology, and the "good life," but not at the expense of religious laws or cultural heritage. Women who have come to the United States with their husbands—who have learned English, dressed in Western clothes, and gone everywhere American wives go with their husbands, say they will return to their traditional role on their return home.

Photograph by John B. Nichol

4

The American In Saudi Arabia

What will happen when you go to Saudi Arabia? Up to now we've been looking rather abstractly at some of the characteristics of Americans and Saudis that make them distinct from one another. Is there any way for you to tell at this point how you will respond to the reality of living in Saudi Arabia or how the Saudis will respond to you? Will the differences we've discussed really be significant? How will they in fact affect specific situations?

Let's see if we can find out. We've recorded in the pages that follow 20 situations or "critical incidents" which may occur in the encounter between Americans and Saudis. They are real events that have happened repeatedly. We're going to describe the incidents, or situations, and then ask you, before reading our comments on them, to think about or discuss what you think the meaning of, or problem in, the situation is. Comparing your reaction with ours will help, we think, to sharpen your appreciation of how culture, values and social customs are likely to be reflected in everyday events during your time in Arabia.

Who's Rude to Whom?
Situation 1

John had only recently arrived in Saudi Arabia to be a production supervisor in a plant his firm was building for the Saudi government.

He had expected things to be different from the States, but he was surprised at how consistently rude the Saudis were, and he was getting tired of it. They came into his office without knocking and started to talk to him even when he was engaged in a conversation with someone else. Then they acted insulted when he told them he was busy and asked them to come back later. In the street he was constantly being brushed and bumped—with no apologies offered. In the bank one day as he waited patiently behind the person at the window for his turn, two Saudis reached rudely past him and urged the teller to take care of their business first.

Discussion of Situation 1

Arabs are very private about their personal lives—but in public, privacy means little. Public space is public—one person has as much right to it as another. In the U.S., we try not to invade someone else's "space"—we even try not to touch each other in a crowded elevator. This is not considered important in Arab countries, and the jostling of crowds on the streets is a part of life.

In personal contacts, such as a visit to the home, traditional Arab hospitality reigns. In impersonal contacts, everyone looks out for himself. There is no queuing up in lines for anything—in the post office, at a restaurant, in a gas station, wherever. Whoever most effectively demands attention, or deserves most respect, will be served first.

Doors are no barrier in an office. An Arab, although he is ceremonious in many other ways, will see no reason to stand on ceremony when entering offices which are considered part of public life. This may stem from the age-old tribal custom of direct petition to the sheik or the king. Even today ordinary citizens may attend the weekly *majlis* held by the King to make complaints, ask favors, seek redress of grievances or simply to renew acquaintance with their chief.

Saudis are offended, though, by brusqueness so try not to show impatience. The best way to react in a situation such as John encountered is to be patient and to give the person suitable attention. Avoid giving the impression of dismissing anyone no matter how busy you may be; it will be counter-productive.

Getting Down to Business
Situation 2

Mr. Jones and Mr. Watson had an appointment with Mr. Mahmoud, a Saudi official, at 10:00 a.m. to discuss some business arrangements. They arrived on time only to be kept waiting for an hour. When they were finally ushered into his office there were several other people in the room.

After serving coffee and engaging in seemingly endless small talk (which was interrupted frequently by the telephone) Mr. Mahmoud finally turned to the Americans and opened up the subject of their visit. As much as Jones and Watson were eager to get on with the serious discussion—which they felt involved rather sensitive and private matters—they were quite hesitant because the other visitors remained in the room within easy listening distance.

Discussion of Situation 2

Saudis do not budget their time in the same way Americans do. Time is a much more flexible commodity in the Arab world. Their evaluation of the use of time is also different. For instance, they consider drinking coffee and chatting in a cafe as "doing something" whereas the Westener usually views it as "doing nothing" and certainly not as an option when "there is work to be done." Nor, in their view, does work have the same intrinsically high value placed upon it by us. Thus most work activities are taken at a leisurely pace. "Haste comes from the devil," according to an ancient Arab proverb, and is therefore avoided. Many Westerners find this difference in pace the most difficult thing to adjust to in Saudi Arabia.

Patience is paramount. Allow more time for an appointment than you think will be necessary, and be prepared to wait. When your time comes (according to *their* sense of time), your Saudi colleague will be very courteous and attentive. He will expect the same of you; showing annoyance will accomplish nothing.

One note of caution: although the Saudi may not always be punctual, they usually expect you, as a foreigner, to be on time.

Saudi Arabians have been engaged in trade since the 7th century, when Mecca was the center of a far-flung trading complex. Saudi businessmen are shrewd and, furthermore, are accustomed to working with Westerners. They conduct business with grace but with no less competitiveness than their foreign counterparts.

Arabs seldom go to the heart of a matter immediately. In opening business (as well as social) conversations, there is always a good-natured and sometimes extensive exchange of pleasantries. We call it "small talk," but to an Arab it is an essential part of hospitality. It also serves to build a relationship before beginning a business discussion.

There is another aspect of the Saudi business meeting that you will find different: your "personal" appointment may take place with a number of other people in the room. As mentioned earlier, Arabs are extremely private in their personal lives, but not in public—and business falls in the public domain. Therefore, although *you* may feel your business is confidential, your Saudi host may not. It is best to relax and accept this custom even though it will require some adjustment on your part. Sip your coffee, chat with everyone, then when the time comes to conduct your business, speak freely. It is a different manner of doing business, but in Saudi Arabia it is the norm.

One Saudi is a Crowd
Situation 3

Joe is a mechanic in charge of equipment maintenance at a large new plant. He had been given the job of instructing a group of Saudis in maintenance procedures. Before long he was ready to give it up; the Saudis were driving him crazy.

"You're gonna come up there some day," he complained to his superior, "and find out I've been trampled to death—or smothered. They stand on top of me, the whole bunch. I can hardly breathe, much less move. They're so close, I hit 'em with the tools when I'm trying to demonstrate something. It gives me the creeps. I can't stand people crowding me like that—and staring—they stare at me like they are wondering how I'd taste roasted over a charcoal fire. I've assigned them seats where I know very well they can hear and see all right, but will they stay put? No siree, there they are the next day crowding up to me again like I was some kind of magnet."

Discussion of Situation 3

The personal distance that is comfortable to people of different cultures varies widely. Saudis may sit or stand closer to you than may be comfortable. But, actually, these Saudis were giving their American instructor the ultimate in courtesy.

Arabs are deeply involved with each other. It is characteristic of them to give the other person complete attention. Thus they stand close and look directly at one another when speaking or listening.

This closeness and continuous eye contact makes many Americans uncomfortable. On the other hand, Arabs who deal with Americans have reported experiencing a certain "flatness" due partly to our very different use of the eyes. In fact, the cocktail party "wandering eye" of many Americans is considered by Arabs to be rude.

Of Skimpy Skirts and Other Dress
Situation 4

Alice, Joe's wife, decided she couldn't just sit in her apartment all day waiting for him to come home so she built up her courage and started out to explore. She'd heard that the *suqs* (marketplaces) sold all kinds of interesting things. In getting dressed she remembered that Saudi women on the streets wrapped themselves up in cloaks so she assumed that one of her relatively short skirts would probably be inappropriate. She put on slacks instead. Because it was so hot, however, she chose to wear a sleeveless tank-top blouse to go with them. Outside, she found a taxi and despite the language barrier managed to communicate her destination.

When she entered the *suq* she was thrilled with the "exotic" atmosphere and began to wander from shop to shop—not saying anything to anybody, just looking. Before long, however, she began to feel quite uncomfortable. Everybody seemed to be staring at her, "undressing her with their eyes," and she was sure they were laughing and making remarks to each other about her even though she couldn't understand what they were saying. Then she realized that a number of the younger men were following her.

Finally, in a panic, she hurried to the street and searched for a taxi to take her back home.

Discussion of Situation 4

Too many American women in Saudi Arabia build walls around themselves and try to pretend that the country doesn't exist. Those who don't, who venture forth to meet the people and to discover what the country has to offer, find it a rewarding experience. They also find it easier if they play by the rules.

One rule relates to dress. Western women aren't expected to wear the *abayah* and veil (and should not), of course, but they *are* expected to acknowledge the country's customs by dressing modestly.

Although Joe's wife recognized that modesty in dress was important, she didn't go far enough. To be sure, short skirts and pants are not appropriate in public (except on the tennis courts), but neither are sleeveless, low-cut or tight-fitting dresses or blouses. Such outfits are especially unacceptable in the bazaars. If you wear slacks, it's best to wear a longsleeved, hip length tunic over them. Hair is also stimulating to Arab men (note that the *abayah* includes a hood which completely covers the hair), so tying on a scarf isn't a bad idea.

Many Western women find full-length skirts or dresses to be the most comfortable when they go out. And many wear the long *thobes* (similar to the garment worn by Arab men) made of colorful cotton. They are cool and comfortable, easy and inexpensive to make—at home or by the *thobe*-makers.

Another rule American women have to be aware of is that they must be careful where they go alone. While a Western woman by herself may take a taxi anywhere in the downtown districts without being concerned, it is better to go in pairs or groups. In no case should she venture too far afield by herself. Nor should a woman go into a restaurant alone, although a group of women may lunch together—so long as they stick to those places frequented by Westerners. Women, even in groups, should not go out on the street by themselves at night.

In other words, the Saudis do not expect Western women to live secluded lives, but neither do they expect them to ignore the customs commonly observed by women in Saudi Arabia.

Brown-Bagging it on Fast Days
Situation 5

Jack Crain and Steve Martin had just arrived in Jiddah where they had jobs with the same company. In general they were satisfied with the work situation except for the annoyance of having to brown-bag it for lunch. It was the middle of Ramadan, when Saudis fast during the day, and no restaurants were open until evening. Personally, they felt it was a little inconsiderate of the Saudis not to keep the restaurants open when there were so many Americans and other non-Muslims around who had to eat. They were also quite bothered by the stares they got from their Saudi co-workers when they stopped for a cigarette break. After all, there was no regulation against smoking in the office!

Discussion of Situation 5

Ramadan, the month of fasting—when eating, drinking and smoking are prohibited between dawn and sunset—is strictly observed. Islam is more than a religion, it's an integral part of the Muslim's social life. Non-Muslims aren't expected to fast, but they should respect the customs of Ramadan by not eating, drinking or smoking in the presence of Muslims.

It is courteous not to smoke on the street or anywhere in public places. Involuntary inhalation of your tobacco smoke may cause a Muslim to break the fast. In any event, it is not easy to observe another doing what is forbidden to you.

Naturally the Arabs eat heartily after sunset and the crowded bazaars are open well into the night. People tend to get less sleep during Ramadan so that as the month progresses, tempers may become short and productivity levels lower.

To Admire or Not to Admire
Situation 6

Mrs. Miles had become acquainted with several Saudi women who spoke enough English to enable her to communicate with them quite well. One day, during the first few months of her stay, she admired a gorgeous emerald ring one of them was wearing. Immediately it was pulled off and thrust onto her own finger. Mrs. Miles naturally returned it with embarrassed protests. On her next meeting with her Saudi friend, she sensed a distinct change in their relationship—a coolness and a distance that hadn't been there before.

Discussion of Situation 6

Visitors are told to be very careful not to admire an Arab's possessions too enthusiastically because you will be given the object immediately no matter how costly it may be. They are further told that if you don't accept the gift, Arabs will feel their friendship has been rejected and feelings will be hurt beyond repair.

This is an exaggeration. True, Arabs consider generosity a corollary of hospitality. Under certain circumstances, such gifts have been and are made. The Saudis may look on this situation in much the same way as we do.

Saudis like to have their possessions admired as much as anyone else. Their innate sense of hospitality and generosity may, however, lead them to offer the admired object as a gift. The proper response is the one we ordinarily would use under such circumstances: If the object is costly, a family heirloom or something equally special, we would naturally express our appreciation but refuse it graciously. (For instance, in the case of the emerald ring, Mrs. Miles could say the ring looked much better on the Saudi lady's hand than on her own.) If the object in question is small, and the circumstances seem right, the gift may be accepted with good grace and thanks.

Letting Them Know What You Think
Situation 7

In America, Bob Green was a supervisor who took no nonsense from any employees who worked under him. His language was "colorful" and he never hesitated to reprimand anyone who performed poorly on the job. His subordinates didn't particularly like him, but they respected him because he was always fair.

Because of his consistently good performance-rating, Bob's company sent him to Saudi Arabia to work in their new plant where he supervised Americans, Saudis and a few workers from other countries. Soon he was complaining to his boss that the Saudis and other Arabs caused more trouble than they were worth and that he continuously had to call them on the carpet—which he did right on the spot so that both the offender and everyone else around would get the message. "But don't worry," he said, "I bawl out the Americans too. I wouldn't show any favoritism. It's just that these Arabs make more trouble and they're getting worse. I may have to really get tough."

Discussion of Situation 7

According to Islamic belief, all are equal in the eyes of Allah. No one is better than anyone else. In practice this means being courteous to and respecting the dignity of everyone, regardless of position. But the issue goes deeper than that. To Arabs, the preservation of dignity and self-respect is an all-important value. Those who lose self-respect, or the respect of others, dishonor both themselves and their families. *Public* criticism is therefore intolerable, since it causes a loss of dignity and denies the respect that is everyone's due. This applies to the way you act toward or speak to anyone—Arab or non-Arab. If you use harsh words, publicly criticize or even contradict a person, Arabs will be hurt on behalf of that person and lose respect for *you*. If you lose the respect of the Saudis around you, your effectiveness with them will be impaired or totally destroyed.

In guarding their personal honor, Saudis may seem hypersensitive, perceiving slights or insults where none are intended. A strong code of courtesy and graciousness in interpersonal relations help Saudis avoid these kinds of misunderstandings.

In this case, it would have been better for Mr. Green to have taken up his complaints privately and tactfully with individual employees rather than critizing them publicly. "Bawling out" an individual, even privately, is considered rude. Mr. Green could have achieved his objective by carefully pointing out the problem and its solution in a positive manner—checking to make sure the Saudis understood him.

The Shutter Bug
Situation 8

Tom was in Saudi Arabia on a special project for several months. While there he was assigned a car and driver to take him wherever he needed to go, including visits to a number of small desert villages outside the city. Since he was fascinated by the contrasts between the traditional and the modern, he took his camera wherever he went so that he could convey to the folks back home what Saudi Arabia was really like.

The driver showed him modern buildings, traffic jams, and the latest technological advances eagerly, but was reluctant when Tom wanted to stop for the more picturesque sights like camels and tents, goats in the streets, the *suqs*, people kneeling in prayer, veiled women, etc. Tom became quite annoyed with his driver. Even more annoying was the fact that most of the people he wanted to photograph turned their backs on him when they saw his camera.

Discussion of Situation 8

It is only comparatively recently that the Kingdom of Saudi Arabia has had the means to build a modern state. The Saudis are proud of the energy and effort they have expended and don't want to appear backward. Understandably, they prefer to show the world those things (modern buildings, automobiles and new roads) that demonstrate the advances that have been made rather than that which foreigners consider "picturesque." This stems not only from pride in their accomplishments but from the expectation that they will be evaluated by Westerners on the degree of modernization that has occurred. The "picturesque" may be viewed as "backward" or different, rather than as a reflection of venerable tradition. Arabs are also sensitive about having pictures taken of women. The basic reason for the resistance to being photographed stems from the Koran prohibition of the depiction of the human form in any way. This ban arises from the idea that man was created in the image of God. One of the laws of Islam forbids the creation of graven images or idols. Applying this in modern life, a photograph of a person is an image.

In some cases, picture-taking is frowned on for security reasons. It's unwise, for example, to take pictures near an airport, or of planes or military installations. In Riyadh or Taif, the summer capital, there are restrictions on photographing the royal palaces or government buildings.

Most of all, make sure your approach is courteous and expresses sincere interest. Do ask permission before you take a picture of anyone. More important, however, is expressing an interest in learning about what you wish to photograph. Tom could have tried to engage his driver in conversation about Saudi traditions. This is an indication of an interest that goes beyond just building a collection of "exotic" snapshots. It is probably impossible (or at best, very difficult) to get the kind of pictures Tom wanted but photographing those scenes recommended by a Saudi results in a collection representative of what Saudis wish to emphasize about their country. You also avoid offending your hosts by clicking away at everything in sight.

Goldbrick or Devotee
Situation 9

Steve had been in Jiddah for several weeks. He hadn't noticed anyone praying in the streets as he'd expected, but he had recently run into a situation that he didn't understand. One of the Saudi men he was supervising had come to him and requested a half-hour for prayer time. Steve was surprised because none of the workers had made such a request during working hours before; but he didn't want to delay his answer while hunting up someone to ask, so he granted the request. He realized, however, that he'd better find out a little more about Muslim prayer times.

Discussion of Situation 9

Muslims are required to pray five times each day. The prayer itself is essentially the same, but there is a prescribed ritual for each prayer which is to be performed at a specific time: at dawn, midday, midafternoon, sunset and nightfall. So the prayers are performed wherever the Muslim might be at the time.

Since the five prescribed prayers are an integral part of life, business hours are adjusted accordingly. Most businesses close during the heat of mid-afternoon so workers usually manage to perform their prayers without interrupting company schedules. Occasionally there are extenuating circumstances, however, and Muslims are never denied the right to prayer time.

Whenever possible, men pray together (inside or outside a mosque) with a selected member of the group leading the prayer. On Fridays (the day of rest) attendance at a mosque is required. The weekly sermon by religious leaders is given at this time.

You will read a lot of "don'ts": Don't step on prayer rugs; don't walk in front of Muslims who are praying; etc., etc. Another "don't" is: *don't* worry too much about all the "don'ts." After all, everyone is quiet and reverent in church—and essentially that's what the prayer rug represents. Deal respectfully with Islam and Muslims in prayer the way you would deal with any other religious activity.

(NOTE: Non-Muslims are not welcome in the mosques or in the religious cities of Mecca and Medina. Do not seek an invitation.)

Although there are no Protestant or Catholic churches in the Kingdom, Saudi Arabia does not prohibit the practice of other religions by the international community.

God and Man in Saudi Arabia
Situation 10

Harry had just been transferred to the office at the Dhahran Airport after several months in Jiddah, the sophisticated port city on the Western Coast of the Arabian Peninsula. The first day he came home in a state of complete exasperation.

"Boy, what a place!" he said to his wife as he collapsed into a chair with a tall drink. "All day long it was *Inshallah. Inshallah. Inshallah.* If I hear one more *"Inshallah"*, I'll go buggy. You'd think everyone was scared of taking responsibility for anything. God may will it, but we're the ones who have to do something about it."

Discussion of Situation 10

Because Islam teaches that all things and all actions are subject to the direct will of God, Saudis have been imbued with a profound sense of the inevitability of events. Nearly every conversation, all references to the future, to what one plans to do or hopes will happen includes the word *"Inshallah"* meaning "if God (Allah) wills it." It is not an empty phrase, despite its frequent use; it is the governing thought. While this attitude may often frustrate Americans who work with Saudis, it sometimes enables Saudis to accept reverses with greater equanimity than Americans.

At the same time, this feeling of inevitability is seldom consciously perceived. Rather, it is a subconscious view of the order of things. This is not to imply that the Saudis take no responsibility for their actions, but rather that they do sincerely believe that no matter how much they personally may want something to take place, and work hard to make it happen, it won't happen if God is not willing.

Inshallah, then, is a cultural reflex. You will find it less irritating if you translate it or interpret it to mean "if possible" or "if all goes well" or "I hope so." It is often a "yes" with a safety valve. In the United States you still hear the comparable phrase: "Yes, God willing."

Inshallah is used more often in the Eastern Province than it is in the western part of the country or even in Riyadh and the central regions.

Smugglers' Due
Situation 11

After a year in Saudi Arabia, Pete and Betty Smith had an opportunity to spend two weeks in Europe on vacation. They so enjoyed eating pork products, that they decided to take some canned bacon and ham back with them packed in with their personal clothing.

The customs officials were very thorough in inspecting all luggage, and the cans were discovered and confiscated.

Discussion of Situation 11

Customs officials in Saudi Arabia watch carefully, just as they do in the United States, for prohibited articles. Regulations are strict and must be obeyed. The law expressly forbids bringing into the country any kind of alcoholic beverages, pork products, narcotics (except those prescribed by a physician), lethal weapons, and literature which is considered pornographic or offensive to the principles of Islam. The Smiths knew this, so they shouldn't have been surprised that the cans were confiscated.

If the Smiths had attempted to carry in alcoholic beverages, even small bottles served on airlines, the penalties might have been even more severe. Even when traveling from place to place within the Kingdom, luggage may be carefully scrutinized. Packing unacceptable items when traveling anywhere is, therefore, unwise.

Alcohol and Ambiguity
Situation 12

Soon after arriving in Saudi Arabia, Max and Esther were invited to dinner at the home of Hasan, a Saudi friend they had known in the States. Hasan welcomed them warmly and served them refreshments—none of which were alcoholic. In the U.S. Hasan had served (and had himself drunk) alcoholic drinks when he had entertained. Max knew that alcohol was illegal in Saudi Arabia, but he also knew the law was winked at. Max wondered if he should ask Hasan for a drink.

Discussion of Situation 12

The use of alcoholic beverages is an area of significant ambiguity in Saudi Arabia. It is forbidden by Islamic law and prohibited by the government. Yet drinking is relatively widespread, especially in the international community. Persons who flout their drinking activities, can get into serious trouble with the police and can anger or embarrass their Saudi friends. One should never *expect* a Saudi to serve liquor. As for Hasan in the U.S., he was observing a U.S. custom.

Drugs are a different matter. Anyone who feels compelled to use any drugs other than those prescribed by a physician should stay out of Saudi Arabia. There is no winking at drug use. Enforcement of drug laws is stringent and users, old or young, risk spending many years in a Saudi jail. If it is necessary for you to carry prescription medication into Saudi Arabia, you should have a letter from your physician stating the name of the drug, and that it is being taken under medical supervision. It is possible to purchase most medication in the Kingdom so carry prescriptions, written in generic terms, for those drugs you may need.

The Inevitable Cup of Coffee

Situation 13

Mr. Bowman, a consulting engineer, found himself in the vicinity of a Saudi colleague's house one evening. Remembering he had a technical question he needed the answer to, he stopped in, intending to stay for only a moment. After a few polite exchanges, Mr. Bowman asked the question he wanted, got the answer and rose to go. Just then a manservant came into the room with a tray on which there were dishes of nuts and something that looked like candy or tiny cookies, as well as a brass coffee pot. Two small cups stood empty beside it. His host insisted that Bowman stay for coffee and refreshments. Bowman really didn't want to stay because he felt he was inconveniencing his host, but he didn't know how to refuse when the tray was placed in front of him.

Discussion of Situation 13

As discussed earlier, undue haste in any social situation (even where "business" is conducted) is frowned on by the Arab. One must take the time to socialize in a more or less prescribed manner, usually somewhat formal and ceremonious. This is true no matter how short the visit. The coffee and/or other refreshments are inevitable. (Remember, you are expected to serve them, when the situation is reversed.)

Arab coffee, which is often flavored with cardamom, is served in small cups—and will continue to be served until you indicate that you have had enough. It is polite to at least sip from a second serving. When you really don't want any more, shaking the cup gently, from side to side, with a twist of the wrist is the "Stop" sign. You'll be understood if you say "No more, thank you" or "Buss," meaning enough. But it will please your host if you follow the cup-shaking custom, done, by the way, only with coffee.)

Coffee may be followed by tea or perhaps a soft drink or fruit juice, especially in the summer months. Tea is somewhat weak, but very sweet, and is occasionally brewed with mint. Sweets and nuts are often offered along with the beverage. On any occasion when food is served, some must be eaten even if you have just come from a full meal.

What Kind of Men Are These
Situation 14

"Hey, this place is mind-blowing," Mark said to his wife when he came home from his work at a construction site in Riyadh one afternoon. They had been in Saudi Arabia only 10 days. "I always thought Arabs were he-men. You know, the way they dominate women and all that. But, I swear, twice today I saw men strolling along holding hands." Here Mark laughed and wiggled a limp wrist at his wife.

Discussion of Situation 14

The Saudi attitude toward contact with members of the same sex differs markedly from the American. It is a common and perfectly acceptable custom in Saudi Arabia, as well as in Mediterranean and other Middle Eastern countries, for men to stroll hand in hand or to greet each other by exchanging a kiss on both cheeks. There are also occasions when they kiss the forehead, the nose or the mouth, depending upon rank, status and relationship. There are no homosexual overtones to this personal contact—instead it fulfills the need for closeness and personal contact in a relationship. Handshaking when meeting friends is a custom Westerners are more accustomed to. In Saudi Arabia any greeting begins by shaking hands and is accompanied among men by many inquiries about the well-being of the friend and his family (without direct reference to his wife).

What's Wrong With Billy?
Situation 15

Linda Rankin learned Saudi ways rather quickly and found shopping in the markets and bazaars quite enjoyable. Unfortunately her twelve-year-old boy, Billy, didn't like going with her. When he did, he kept his hands in his pockets, would never touch anything, and was even reluctant to help her carry the packages of things she bought.

She finally confronted him one day after a particularly frustrating morning of trying to get him to behave normally.

Finally he burst out crying. "They'll think I'm stealing something and cut my hands off," he said through his tears.

Discussion of Situation 15

We have all heard many tales about what might happen to us in Arab countries, especially Saudi Arabia, if we should break the law, even in ignorance. "Thieves get their hands cut off and criminals are beheaded in the public square." These things do happen, but their significance, especially for the Western visitor, is exaggerated. Let's look at Saudi crime and punishment a little more closely.

Saudi justice is based on religious law, and the Koran stipulates the punishment for most crimes. The Saudis strictly enforce their beliefs and are quick to deal severely with wrongdoers. As a result, the crime rate is low and one should feel safer in Saudi Arabia than in many other places in the world.

It is true that there are occasions when a thief has had a hand cut off. Public executions sometimes occur; the assassin of King Faisal was beheaded in June of 1975, while thousands in Riyadh watched (which is not all that different from American T.V. cameras following a convicted criminal into the death chamber). It is also true that in Saudi Arabia, as in America, ignorance of the law is no excuse. For the most part, however, the religious judges (*qadis*) tend to be just and humane in their case-by-case interpretation of the law.

The point is, if you look for trouble, you can always find it. Americans *are* subject to Saudi law, though generally speaking Saudi officials are less punitive with foreigners than they are with their own people. The most frequent offenses by Americans are drug or alcohol violations. Some have served prison sentences; some have been deported.

However, while the punishment for a Westerner may be less severe, a foreigner involved in an incident, such as a traffic accident, with a Saudi will always be found at fault. This is true even if you are stopped at a traffic light and are hit from behind. The reasoning behind this is: "If you had not been there, it wouldn't have happened!"

If you are an ordinary law-abiding citizen obeying the customs and laws to the best of your ability, you'll get along just as well in Saudi Arabia as at home.

Beware of Assumptions
Situation 16

Charley Sands was assigned to the Kingdom to train young Saudi mechanics in the repair and maintenance of newly imported road building equipment. Much of the training had focused on the effective use of the maintenance manuals prepared by the manufacturer. The training program went smoothly enough, but later, during his follow-up inspection, Charley discovered that the machinery had fallen into disrepair. On inquiry he learned that despite the training, the maintenance manual was rarely consulted by the Saudi mechanics. This caused a great deal of hair-pulling in the American company headquarters, but no one could figure out what to do about it.

Discussion of Situation 16

Western countries and Saudia Arabia are engaged in a rapid and extensive transfer of technology. Often ignored, however, is the fact that there are certain basic Western values and assumptions about the nature of human beings and the world they live in which underlie technological development. When technology is transferred to non-Western cultures, these assumptions come along with it and frequently conflict with values and assumptions in the host society (although in some cases, for example Japan, the host society has been quite receptive).

Modern technology is premised on the assumption that reality can be dealt with by a series of prescribed steps based on a plan, on an abstract design, or on a set of concepts which can be used as a guide. It is assumed, for example, that directions will be provided and carefully followed since it is "understood" that machines will work properly only if they are serviced regularly. For Saudis such a guide is an ideal that does not necessarily translate into reality. Reality is disorderly and heavily dependent on chance or the will of God. The Saudi is thus less likely to follow a handbook or a design than to deal with each situation as it arises. More patience and effort is needed in helping the Saudi understand the practical use of the handbook.

Different training and supervisory techniques will be required. Reading and lecturing about the necessary procedures and the reasons for them are rarely an effective training method for people who have not had the same kind of experience with machinery as Westerners. The problems that will occur if procedures are *not* followed must be illustrated, perhaps with cartoon character films showing how injuries can be avoided by using proper care and following safety precautions. These procedures will have to be gone over many times using a variety of teaching methods.

There are other cultural assumptions embedded in technology: that it is acceptable to divide or fragment labor so that a team of people doing different things can produce a single unified end product or that time involves a simple linear progression and is divisible into rigidly discrete segments. The average Saudi is not very comfortable with either of these concepts. He is extremely individualistic and time for him flows in a less easily segmented manner.

A recognition that cultural assumptions come along with technology will help Americans better understand and be more patient in the process of transfer.

Saudi Guests

Situation 17

Carl had become quite friendly with a couple of Saudis in his section at the plant and had invited them home to dinner. He had mentioned that his wife was anxious to meet their wives. By this he meant, of course, that their wives were invited too. But when the men arrived, each came alone, about an hour late.

By then Carl's wife was quite distressed. First, she had prepared dinner for six. Second, because she knew drinking was prohibited, she had planned dinner to be ready shortly after 7:00 p.m. when the guests were expected to arrive. She was certain the meal was ruined. Trying to make the best of it, she suggested the men remove their headdresses in order to be more comfortable and invited them to the table at once.

Discussion of Situation 17

Although the custom is changing gradually among the younger and Western-educated Saudis, for the most part separation of men and women is still the rule. Therefore, don't be surprised if, when inviting a Saudi couple to your home, only the man comes. You can be more specific when extending the invitation by suggesting that his wife is welcome, allowing him the opportunity to accept or not on her behalf.

When entertaining Saudis in your home, always take time for the initial period of conversation and serve coffee, tea or a fruit drink as soon as they arrive. Contrary to our custom, conversation and coffee come first; the meal is at the end of the evening and guests leave soon after the after-dinner coffee is drunk.

The normal dinner hour for Saudis is later than most Americans are accustomed to (remember that there are prayers to be said at sunset) and attitudes toward time are different. Being "on time" in Saudi Arabia can easily mean arriving an hour later than expected. A more casual approach to preparing and serving meals is called for.

Some other things to keep in mind:

Offer extra servings of food more than once. Arabs normally refuse the first time out of politeness. If your offer isn't accepted after a second or third time, then you may feel sure they really don't want any more.

In conversing with Arabs (as in supervising their work) try not to show impatience, preoccupation with other affairs or undue haste. Impatience is considered a sign of bad manners or a lack of self-confidence.

It is customary to greet senior guests at the door of their car and to accompany all visitors at least to the door of your home (or office), and sometimes to the street or car when they depart. The Arab's protest that his host remain comfortably seated in the office or living room is largely a formality.

Remember that the American habit of relaxing in a chair with the legs crossed, so that the soles of the shoes face the person opposite you, may offend the Saudi. This is more likely to be of concern in the rural or more conservative areas than in the cities. The more "Westernized" Saudis you will meet may understand that you are not deliberately insulting them. But it would be courteous if you sat with the soles of your shoes on the floor.

It is perfectly proper for an Arab to wear his headdress indoors. He may prefer to. If he'd rather remove it, he will do so.

What Happens in a Saudi Home?
Situation 18

Dick and Mary Johnson had been in Jiddah for several months, where Dick was working as an airline pilot. He had become quite friendly with Hassan who invited him to his home for dinner. Hassan had specifically included Mary in the invitation, even though he had never met her and, of course, the Johnsons hadn't met Hassan's family.

Dick had accepted the invitation, and they were looking forward to being in a Saudi home; but they were also a little worried about what would happen and what would be expected of them: Would Hassan's wife be there? If not, would Mary be allowed to stay with Dick and Hassan, or would she have to go to the "women's quarters"? She didn't speak Arabic. Would Hassan's wife speak English? Would they have to sit on the floor? Would they have knives and forks? Or would they be expected to eat with their hands? Was she supposed to take a gift? Should they keep their shoes on or remove them? And what would they talk about? Perplexed by these questions, they almost wished they hadn't accepted the invitation.

Discussion of Situation 18

Saudis are friendly, hospitable, generous people. If you should be invited to their homes, don't pass up the opportunity. Try to follow their social customs, but relax about it. Saudis are used to foreigners and are tolerant of mistakes made in good faith.

Again, it must be stressed that although customs are changing in Saudi Arabia, it is not happening overnight. Separation of men and women remains the rule, even to the extent that many houses still have separate entrances and separate reception rooms for men and women. If invited to dinner, an American man *may* be expected to enter one doorway while his wife enters another leading to the "women's quarters." Among older Saudis the normal procedure is for men to be invited to dine with Saudi men, with the women not included at all.

There are several possibilities and you should be prepared to meet any of them:

—The wife may not be invited at all
—She may be invited but be expected to go directly to the women's quarters
—She may be included at dinner with the men, but the Saudi wife may not appear
—The Saudi wife may be included
—If included, the Saudi wife may or may not be veiled in the presence of a man outside her immediate family

In the cities—and especially among Western-educated Saudis and those who deal regularly with foreigners—the practice of men and women entertaining and being entertained together is increasing. Although Saudi women don't mix with men in public gatherings, and still wear the *abayah* and veil in public, you will see them more and more in very fashionable Western clothes and without the veil at private parties. Western women should remember to dress modestly, even in these circumstances.

In any case, among the Saudis you are likely to meet, American wives will probably not be isolated in the company of the Saudi women if she doesn't speak Arabic and they don't speak English.

All Arabs enjoy good conversation. It is likely to be spirited and good-natured, but wisecracking and barnyard humor are inappropriate. There's a great deal of pleasant small talk in the beginning. A good opener is to ask about the health and well-being of the other person. In male gatherings, it's best not to mention wives or women relatives specifically. (The American "How's the wife?" is not appropriate.) Inquire about his work, some interest you know he has, or make a complimentary remark about the local soccer team. Family affairs are considered private. A Saudi will rarely talk about his children until he has known you for some time—nor will he want to hear about your children or their latest activities.

It has been said that religion and politics should not be discussed at social gatherings with Saudis. Actually, there are few conversational taboos. The Saudis you will meet will be able and eager to talk about a wide variety of topics. However, a Westerner should not express anything critical or downgrading about the Kingdom, Islam or the mid-Eastern political situation.

Most Saudis with whom foreigners come in contact are likely to serve a meal in much the same manner as dinners are served in the West, with conventional tables and chairs, knives and forks. We've all heard the admonition not to take or offer food or drink with the left hand. While this is true, left-handed persons need not anticipate embarrassment when holding their fork in their left hand.

You *may* be lucky enough to be invited to a dinner served on the floor in the "traditional" manner and eaten by hand. In this case, do not use the left hand. (Remember this is the "unclean" hand in Saudi tradition. Think how hard it must have been to wash one's hands in the desert and you will easily understand how this has become a deeply ingrained custom.) For the same reason, try not to sit in such a way that the soles of your shoes will face someone directly. Tuck your feet under you or sit cross-legged, rather than stretching them out.

After coffee or tea is served, the dinner is over and it's time for guests to leave.

It is safest not to smoke at the table unless your host sets the example. Most Saudis do not like it. Watch for other behavior clues. For example, many Saudis remove their shoes upon entering their homes. If your host and other guests do so, remove yours also. (In many homes it is quite customary to sit on the floor, and shoes are removed to keep the rugs cleaner.)

Only on rare occasions will the foreigner have the opportunity to enjoy a traditional Arab feast. If you are invited to one—perhaps a picnic or beach party—rejoice. It may be served on mats or rugs on the ground or floor, though tables and chairs are often used. The meal is usually an elaborate affair. A great variety of food will be served. Water, soap and towels will be passed; then rosewater will be poured over the hands. More coffee will be served, and often a burner of incense will be passed around for the guests to inhale and waft into their beards and clothes. This final rite is a sign that the guests may take their leave.

As far as gifts are concerned, the practice is much the same as it is in the U.S. If you are invited to someone's home for dinner or a party, it is courteous to take a small gift along or send it the next day with your thank-you note; but there is no hard and fast rule about it. A thank-you note should always be sent.

Abigail's Anxieties

Situation 19

Abigail was beginning to feel sorry for herself; she and her husband, Terry, had been in Saudi Arabia for only a few months, but what she had to put up with!

The street outside their home had been torn up—it seemed forever—and the dust and sand seeped into everything. Her husband had the car all day, though she wouldn't have been permitted to drive it anyway. It was annoying, and she resented having to depend on him to take her everywhere, even shopping. But now she had come to the end of her rope. With six people coming to dinner, she had just discovered that the gas bottle was empty and they had no phone! *Now* what was she supposed to do?

Discussion of Situation 19

Living in Saudi Arabia is not going to be easy if you insist on running your life and your household according to the standards to which you have been accustomed. But "necessity is the mother of invention," and a little flexibility mixed with a generous sense of humor will help immeasurably.

First of all, accept the fact that in rapidly growing cities certain problems are inevitable: there is construction everywhere; houses are going up faster than streets can be paved; all utilities are taxed beyond capacity; supply cannot keep up with demand; practically everything has to be imported and delays are inevitable. Heat, humidity and sand are hard on appliances and all working parts of all types of machinery, and a shortage of craft skills and parts makes it hard to get things repaired in a hurry. The Saudis don't "enjoy" these inconveniences either, but they accept them. So—use a little American ingenuity.

Most cooking is done with bottled gas. Sometimes there are no gauges or the gauges don't work. If you put your mind to it, however, you can probably devise some way to estimate when the bottle will run out—or keep a spare on hand. Be prepared with alternative methods of cooking: small electric appliances, a charcoal grill, an hibachi, etc. If worse comes to worst, you can always eat out. Some Lebanese-style restaurants offer "carry-out" service for hors d'oeuvres and entrees.

Since your electricity may go out—due to a sandstorm, construction cut-offs or other causes—keep a supply of candles or flashlights on hand.

You may have planned a menu around roast beef only to discover that there are no good roasts in the market that day. Because of transportation schedules, the availability of food items and other supplies fluctuates. So it is wise to stock up on staples when they are available and plan your meals around whatever fresh foods *are* in the markets. Beef or chicken—does it really matter? And don't be a slave to imported foods. Try local products and learn to use them in the special dishes of the area. If you do shop in the *suqs,* be ready to bargain. In other shopping places, the price quoted should be paid but in the *sugs* the announced price is rarely the selling price. Bargaining is expected; it is a social exchange between customer and proprietor.

If the man in the family goes on a trip out of the Kingdom, plan ahead. Stock up on supplies, get an extra bottle of gas, arrange with another family to check in with you periodically while he's gone in case of emergencies.

Probably the hardest thing for a woman to get used to is not being able to jump in the car or pick up the telephone and call whomever she wants.

If your house has a phone, rejoice—but be patient with its limitations. Phone service is relatively new and not fully developed. It's often easier to call the U.S. than next door. If your house doesn't have a phone, don't expect to have one installed the next day. There just aren't that many available, but it's not the end of the world. You may wish to visit people in the evening to personally set dates. Or messages may be phoned from the husband's office. Check around to find the nearest neighbor with a phone. Most communications and invitations are in the form of notes. A good supply of informal stationery is a must.

Taxis are plentiful in most areas and may be flagged down on the street. Don't be surprised if, after you have finally succeeded in flagging down a cab, a Saudi steps in front of you and gets into the taxi. This is not rudeness—again, it is the Saudi way of life. Trustworthy drivers are available for hire. You may be able to arrange with some neighboring families to hire a driver jointly. Women will find many things easier to do if they do them in the company of one or two other women.

Women will also have to accept the fact that they will have to rely on their husbands to take care of many household details (like calling someone to fix a broken water pipe) that they are used to handling themselves, and for transportation.

Remember, everyone else is coping or has coped with the same frustrations. Talk with people who have been in the country for awhile to find out how they do things. But a word of caution: many people, for personal reasons, find it difficult to adjust to a foreign country. Unfortunately, some excuse themselves by laying all the blame on their hosts. Be wary of these kinds of people. The prejudices and stereotypes they have will be of very little help to you.

Terry's Tribulations

Situation 20

While Abigail was bemoaning her difficulties at home, Terry was sitting in his office thinking about his own problems.

He considered himself a very efficient administrator as well as an expert civil engineer. That was why he was chosen for this job. But he was finding it very difficult to run a "tight ship" as he had back in the States. The business of the shoes was particularly annoying. The company provided coveralls and safety shoes to all the plant workers. The men nodded and smiled graciously when the garments were given to them, but not one of them would wear the shoes, even though Terry reminded them every day. They insisted on wearing the sandals that almost everyone in Saudi Arabia wore, but which didn't offer enough protection to their feet around heavy equipment. He was sure somebody would get hurt one of these days.

Then there were all the things he continuously had to remember to do for his wife—things she had always taken care of back home. She had exploded the other day when he'd forgotten to call the water company about filling their water tank.

"Oh, boy," he thought suddenly, reaching for the phone, "I forgot to call Tom to get a message to Janice that Abbey wants to go shopping with her tomorrow."

Discussion of Situation 20

The traditions of centuries cannot be changed overnight, neither in Saudi Arabia nor anywhere else—even in so simple a matter as wearing more practical footwear. Terry was suggesting a new way that didn't make sense to Saudis who had been successfully doing things in their own way for many years. Not wishing to insult or embarrass Terry, the clothing was accepted but this did not guarantee it would be used. As with procedures for operating machinery, safety precautions (and the consequences of ignoring them) must be presented many times using a variety of methods to help the workers understand their importance.

As for household chores, American husbands in Saudi Arabia simply have to get used to doing many things previously done by their wives in the U.S. It can sometimes be annoying to include these tasks in an already busy day or arrive home to the chore of changing the gas bottle. A sense of humor is handy in these situations, and packing a well-equipped tool kit is a necessity.

These situations and the commentary on them are offered as a basic practical guide to Saudi-American social relations. After you have been in Saudi Arabia for several months, re-read this section (indeed, a re-reading of the entire book will produce some startling revelations) and compare our discussion with your own experiences—see how many actually arise in your social, family or business relationships.

5

Culture Shock and the Adjustment of Lifestyles

You are probably familiar with the term "culture shock," though you may not be clear as to its precise meaning.

Basically, culture shock refers to the personal dislocation and sense of disorientation that people experience when they go to live in a new and different environment—most often a foreign country. It does not necessarily mean being put off by the differences that are encountered. Often it is merely a sense of "being out of step" and unsure about how to handle even the simple things in life. Given our ingrained ways of doing and seeing things—our unconscious expectations about how people should behave and how the physical and social environment should be ordered—it is no small wonder that problems arise.

The problems are called culture shock and stem from the loss of the thousands of familiar clues and cues which in your own society tell you, in any given situation, who you are, what you should do and how you should communicate. It is hard to understand the role these cues play in making you comfortable when you are at home—until you're deprived of them and forced to decipher a whole set of new ones.

We won't go into detail here about the symptoms of culture shock.[1] They include hyper-

---

[1] For a fuller discussion of culture shock see Kohls, L. Robert, *Survival Kit, for Overseas Living*. Chicago, Illinois: Intercultural Press, Inc., 1979, P. 62-70.

irritability, bitterness, resentment, homesickness, depression and psychosomatic illnesses—and all too often excessive drinking. Almost everyone suffers from culture shock in one degree or another, some so severely that they are forced to return home before the completion of their assignment.

The important thing is to know what the antidotes are. One antidote is to devote time and effort to understanding the difference between your own customs and values and those of your hosts, in this case the Saudis. Be alert to areas of conflict or misunderstanding, and exercise the patience, openness and tolerance needed to build bridges between yourself and your hosts.

Another antidote is to take a positive attitude toward the development of a lifestyle in Saudi Arabia that will meet your needs and those of your family—while being ready to accept the fact that it will have to be essentially on Saudi terms. Some people isolate themselves in little enclaves (ghettos) of Americans and manage to avoid some of the difficulties inherent in living in Saudi Arabia. In doing so, however, they miss the richness of the experience, often becoming discontented and unjustifiably resentful toward the Saudis—who after all are simply being themselves.

We adapt and adjust not simply to please or to avoid offending the Saudis, but because it also makes for a more satisfying personal experience and greater efficiency and effectiveness in accomplishing the jobs we are there to do.

Finally, emphasis needs to be placed on the *active phase* of adjustment. A negative, passive response to the sense of disorientation you may feel is the surest way to make it worse.

This and the following chapter, then, will discuss ways in which you can take the initiative in developing a lifestyle adapted to both you *and* Saudi Arabia. The first thing you want to do, the comments above notwithstanding, is to find ways to pursue the kinds of interests and activities you enjoy at home. This does not, of course, mean trying to recreate America in the middle of the Arabian desert, but it means being ready to take advantage of the opportunities that are there. You may not always be able to do things *in the same way* that you do them at home, but finding similar activities is almost always possible.

First you need to take a close look at what you really like. Your lifestyle is composed of habit patterns adapted to the trappings of your own culture and environment. When these trappings are removed you may be at a loss not only to satisfy your needs, but even to define clearly just what they are.

What comes to mind when you hear the word "lifestyle?" In what terms would you describe your own?

- A house, two cars, country club membership, summer camp for the kids?
- Apartment with a swimming pool, symphony concerts and the theater, plenty of time for reading?
- Office work at home most evenings, the ball game on TV Saturday afternoons, Sunday with the children, dinner out once a week?
- Weekly bridge luncheon, volunteer work at the hospital, family get-togethers for Sunday dinner?
- Cocktail parties, the races, skiing vacations?
- Camping and hiking, swimming parties at the lake?

And what is it that determines a person's lifestyle? "Money" seems like the obvious answer, but culture and the behavior patterns of the groups with which we identify are just as strong an influence on our lifestyle choices as money.

These choices are culturally and environmentally influenced without our being aware of it. For instance, climate has a lot to do with our choices of food, shelter, clothing and, to some extent, our social or leisure-time activities. Religion and education, by influencing what we think and believe, also have an influence on what we do.

As you move to Saudi Arabia, however, or into any other culture where the lifestyle choices are at least different if not more limited, it is important to become consciously aware of the various aspects of your present situation and to assess how important each is to you.

This is the first step in "adjusting" to living in Saudi Arabia. Here are a few ideas to help you.

Determining Your Lifestyle Preferences

Drawing a profile of your personal lifestyle will help you predict and understand the frustrations you may face when and if certain things are no longer available to you and will help you figure out in *advance* what alternatives you should provide.

This exercise will help you pinpoint what is important to you—what you really like to do, what makes you happy and what annoys you, whether you are dependent on others or are a free and independent spirit.

1. Make a list of all the things you can think of that you like, that give you pleasure—from drinking with the boys, eating Polynesian food and entertaining to making new friends, going to the movies and participating in church work.
2. Take a good look at each item you've written down and think carefully about how important it is to you (what kind of physical or emotional satisfaction you get from it). Cross off those items that you decide aren't really important to you and which you don't really feel strongly about.

3. Sort out the remaining and list them in the order of their importance under three headings:

Things I value highly and that I do regularly:	*Things I do when and if I find the time:*	*Things I don't do often but would like to do:*
Example: Golf	Example: Reading	Example: Gardening

Record the first list in the left-hand column of the *Personal Lifestyle Profile—First Priority* below and the other two lists in the appropriate columns of the *Personal Lifestyle Profile—Second and Third Priorities*.

You now have an outline profile of your lifestyle preferences. The next step is to gather data on what is available or permissible in Saudi Arabis that will enable you to satisfy your first priority preferences. Indicate availability in the column to the right of each item. Then from the second and third lists ("Things I do when I find time" and "Things I would like to do") record in the right-hand column of the first priority list things that are available in Saudi Arabia which might substitute for the things you most like to do but cannot. Finally, when you finish identifying alternatives from your second and third priority lists, begin working on "Uniquely Saudi List."

Place in this list those things that are available to do in Saudi Arabia which you cannot do in the U.S. Your exploration of alternatives for the first three priority lists will quite likely provide material for this list. In addition, you may want to write in some activities that will be necessary in Saudi Arabia, such as (for husbands) running errands for and chauffering wives, (for wives) advance planning for stocking household necessities and (for both) personal visits with friends to plan social events.

It is not the purpose of this handbook to provide all the detailed information you will need to complete this exercise. Some is included in the material which follows. We suggest, books on Saudi Arabia in print. A sample selection is listed in the resources section on page   . Also talk with acquaintances who have been there (or with Saudi Government personnel or students, educators or businessmen visiting the U.S.). Above all, keep this book handy and return to the exercise once you have settled in.

PERSONAL LIFESTYLE PROFILE—FIRST PRIORTY

In order of importance to me, these are things I value highly and do regularly:	Available in S.A. (yes/no)	Substitutions for things not available in Saudi Arabia: (See Second and Third Priority List and Uniquely Saudi List.)

SECOND AND THIRD PRIORITY LIFESTYLE PREFERENCES

II. Things I Like To Do When And If I Find Time:	Available in S.A. (yes/no)	III. Things I Don't Do Now But Would Like to Try:	Available in S.A. (yes/no)

CULTURE SHOCK AND THE ADJUSTMENT OF LIFESTYLES / 73

UNIQUELY SAUDI LIST

ACTIVITIES/EVENTS etc. available in Saudi Arabia and *not* available in U.S.

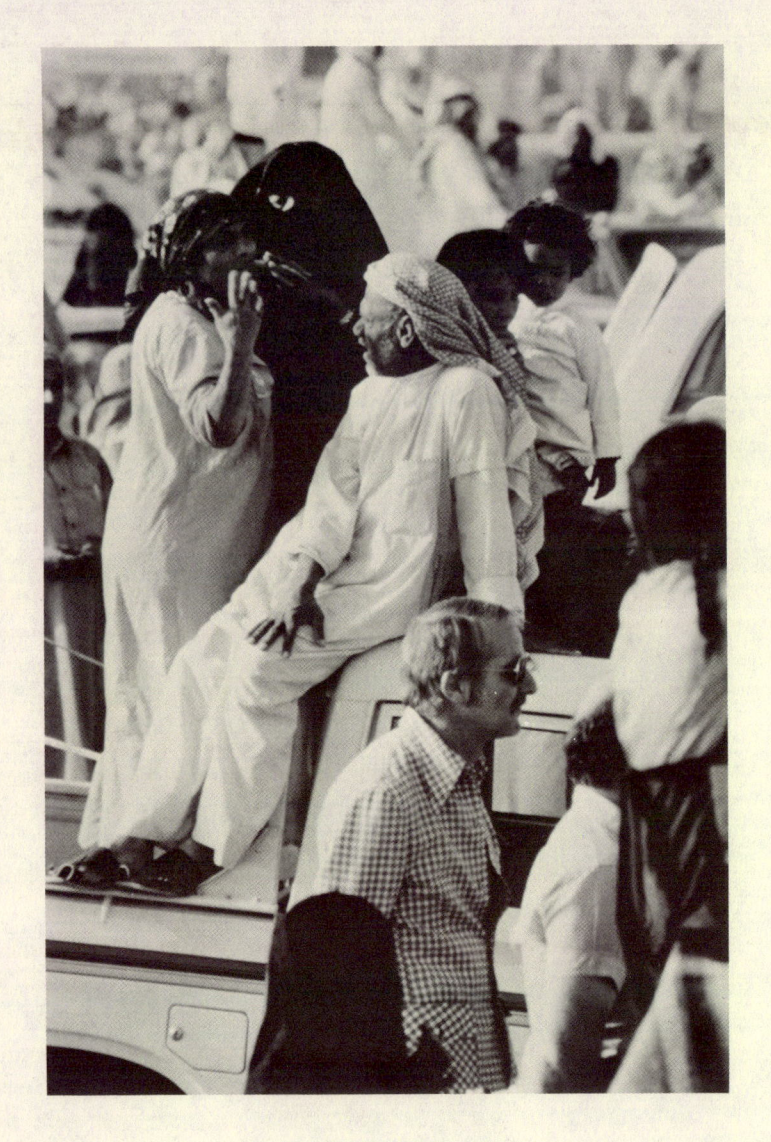

Photograph by John B. Nichol

6

ENJOYING YOURSELF IN SAUDI ARABIA

Saudi Arabia offers much that is interesting for people who are not dependent entirely on outside stimuli. Public entertainment is practically non-existent. There are no movies, theaters, concerts, night-clubs or bars—except as provided within American or other foreign compounds or clubs. You will find plenty to do, however, if you make the effort to search it out.

Women in particular will have to take the initiative. Although a few American wives work, most do not. Opportunities are limited. With their husbands and children occupied during the day, women often fall prey to loneliness and boredom. At the outset, lack of mobility will also be a problem since women (Saudi or foreign) are not permitted to drive in the Kingdom. In the words of one American woman:

At first it is hard to get used to—not being able to jump into a car and take off at a moment's notice. But you *do* get used to it. Taxis are everywhere and many companies have bus transport for their people. Besides, quite a few families that live near each other work out a system of shared drivers so there is likely to be one available any time you want him.

It is also hard on single men and teenagers, with the limited access to movies and other entertainment, and the total lack of dating opportunities, alcoholic beverages, etc. With a little thought and effort, the problem of "what to do" can be solved.

The specific activities mentioned in this section refer to Jiddah and Riyadh for the most part, but can be used as a guide for searching out things to do in any of the major cities.

Jiddah is a cosmopolitan city, having for centuries been host to Muslim pilgrims from all over the world. With the foreign embassies located there, it is also a lively place socially.

Riyadh (pronounced Ree-odd), the Royal Capital, is more conservative and more traditional than the coastal cities. But tradition and progress stand side by side. It is growing rapidly and expects to host the foreign embassies in due time.

Dhahran is the oil capital of Saudi Arabia and has been the headquarters for the Arabian-American Oil Company for the past 40 years. It is actually not a city at all; the area includes the Dhahran International Airport, the University of Petroleum and Minerals, the U.S. Consulate General and several company compounds, as well as Aramco's installations. ("Straight out of Pasadena!" one American said of the company compounds.) The thousands of foreigners who live and work in the area have Dhahran as a postal address, although they actually may live in the neighboring cities of al-Khubar and Dammam.

Here are some suggested "things-to-do" to consider incorporating into your lifestyle plan:

Most *entertaining* centers around events that can be organized in your home. They will be similar to those enjoyed in the U.S. depending on your preferences. Cook-outs, game or card parties, brunches, formal dinners are all possible.

As you make Saudi friends, they too will enjoy being invited to your home—as you will enjoy going to theirs.

More and more restaurants are appearing in Saudi Arabia's cities. They are fairly expensive, but offer a wide variety. In Jiddah, for instance,

Chinese, Pakistani, Lebanese, Korean, Indonesian and Turkish cuisines as well as Arab and American are available. There are also several good local fast food places in both Jiddah and Riyadh. Chicken roasted on a spit or a *shawarma* sandwich (roasted meat in a fresh roll) with salad and *tahinah* (sesame) sauce make good take-home food or picnic fare. Hamburgers and Kentucky Fried Chicken are also available.

In Jiddah there are many *embassy affairs* to which you may be invited.

If you enjoy concerts, plays, etc., plan to provide your own *cultural entertainment*. Take along your stereo equipment and your favorite records and tapes. Because of heat, humidity and dust, tapes fare better than records.

Take along your musical instruments. Evenings of music and play and poetry reading are popular. There are organized musical and dramatic groups in the larger cities, both amateur and professional.

In Jiddah, the international community has created the Hejaz Choral Society, The Jiddah Players and the Saudi Equity Theater which give professional performances. In Riyadh, the Riyadh Amateur Little Theater produces plays and each spring stages the Desert Horse Opera which combines riding and acting. These groups always welcome new members.

Although *movies* are in a gray area of approval, they are permitted in Western compounds and are privately sponsored by many U.S. companies.

Saudi *television* stations provide both educational and entertainment programs, but the bill of fare is limited. There are some English-language programs, but naturally most programming is designed for the Saudi audience. American TV sets won't work in Saudi Arabia without alteration to the European system, so it's best in the long run to buy your set in the Kingdom. One that takes video cassettes enables you to program your own TV and movie schedule.

If you have a *hobby*—or if you have a list of things you've always wished you had time to do—now is the time. Painting? Macrame? Leathercraft? Whatever. Take with you the equipment you will need. If you are accomplished in any craft, you might want to offer a class.

If you like to *sew,* take along your sewing machine. Fabrics are lovely, available and inexpensive, but bring your own patterns.

Playing games and putting together puzzles are activities that can be enjoyed by the family or at parties. It will be necessary to take an abundant supply of both for children and adults. Games are often played at adult parties.

Celebrating American holidays can be very important when you are living in another country. Preparations for doing so must begin at home because supplies for Thanksgiving, Halloween, birthdays and Christmas celebrations must be shipped. No religious articles of any description can be imported into Saudi Arabia, but a small artificial Christmas tree and non-religious decorations (balls, strings of lights, tinsel) can be shipped. You may want to carry a stack of holiday paper plates, cups and napkins and some decorations to make these occasions festive.

Learn the art of *gourmet cooking.* Try the exotic foodstuffs in the local markets. (Take along a metric scale as well as sets of measuring cups and spoons.)

Now's the time, too, to catch up on your *reading*—all those books you've been meaning to get to. Several embassies in Jiddah maintain lending libraries—as do the English-Language Center and British Council in Riyadh. There are also book-stores, but with a limited selection of

English-language books. Bring with you the books you know you want to read. The *International Herald Tribune,* the international edition of American weekly news magazines (*Newsweek, Time,* etc.) and European newspapers are sold in the bookstores and hotels. There are two English-language newspapers published in Jiddah, the *Arab News* and the *Arab Gazette.*

Gardening, both indoor and outdoor, is a popular pastime. There are several good nursery and garden shops in both Jiddah and Riyadh, and there are gardeners for hire.

Shopping, particularly in the bazaars (*sugs*), is often a social activity in itself. After sundown, during Ramadan especially, the *sugs* can be very gay and lively places, full of goods not seen at any other time of year.

The Riyadh *Zoo and Botanical Gardens* provide popular entertainment. There are specified days for men and women, but Western families are usually allowed to attend on men's days (except Fridays, the Muslim Sabbath).

Fine beaches line both the east and west coasts of the Arabian peninsula. *Water sports*—swimming, sailing, fishing, waterskiing, snorkeling, scuba-diving, shelling—are possible all year round. Take any equipment you need for these activities with you.

Abhor Creek, about 20 minutes by car from Jiddah, is a popular recreation area for water sports. Villas, cottages or cabanas may be rented, although the demand is greater than the supply. The Red Sea Sailing Association has a clubhouse and small marina there. The Red Sea itself offers excellent deep-sea fishing and skin diving. Again, take along your own equipment, as the proper reel and lines are not available there.

There are a number of swimming pools available in both Jiddah and Riyadh. Single and season tickets may be purchased for pool swimming at several of the hotels.

Horseback riding is popular and available to both men and women everywhere in Saudi Arabia. There are riding clubs in all major cities, with competitive trials as well as riding for fun. Stables board and rent horses, provide riding instruction and hold frequent shows. If you are a serious rider, bring your gear.

The Al-Hamdami Riding Association is the center of activity in Jiddah and there are two riding clubs in Riyadh.

Other sports include tennis, baseball, softball, volleyball, football, cricket and badminton. The Dunes Club, at the American Embassy in Jiddah, offers squash, tennis and golf; contact the Embassy for membership.

Soccer is the most popular local *spectator sport,* with matches most Fridays, though women rarely attend.

There is a racing club in Riyadh which presents not only horse-racing but also 2600-meter camel races. (Although there is no betting allowed, cash prizes are presented.) Western women rarely attend.

Women may attend all ball games, etc., within the international community.

Camping and picnicking are both popular and may be combined with trips to cultural and historical sites. Camping and picnic equipment are available in the markets, but if you are a camping enthusiast by all means bring along your own. A large cooler, for picnics, is an invaluable addition to your shipment.

North of Jiddah, about three-and-a-half-hours' driving time, near the Coast Guard Station, are the ruins of an early Islamic trading port called Jar. Madain Salih, the ruins of an ancient Nabatean city with inscriptions dating back to the first Century B.C., is about 200 miles north of Medina. Permission must be obtained from the Government to visit there.

South of Jiddah, the cities of Abha, Bisha, Najran and al-Qaraah are of cultural and historical interest. A former royal palace stands at al-Qaraah.

Desert picnics are popular in Riyadh in the cool fall and spring days. There are many places close by, off both the Jiddah and Dhahran Roads. Interesting rock and fossil specimens may be found on these jaunts.

Other popular sites for picnicking and camping in the Riyadh area include the petrified forest east of the city on the Damman Road and the Tuwayq Escarpment along the Mecca Road.

In the Eastern Province there are many oases and archeological sites. In the Dhahran area, the best nearby sites for desert camping trips are the escarpments and limestone out-croppings off the Abqaiq-Hofuf Road.

A trip in the desert—either a picnic or a longer expedition—can be a tremendously exciting experience. BUT DO NOT TACKLE IT ON YOUR OWN. Obtain advice and guidance. You might want to contact the Natural History Society in Jiddah as a starter. They arrange desert field trips and have the necessary experience, guides and equipment.

Develop the art of *sight-seeing*. A walk through the teeming markets of the towns and through the palm groves of the oases, where traditional ways of life seem to be timeless, is a fascinating way to discover many facets of Arabian life.

In Jiddah, a walking tour of the old city—especially interesting in the late afternoon when the lamplighters are at work—will allow you to step back in time.

Although you may not enter the city of Mecca (unless you are a Muslim), the trip to Taif, the Government's summer capital in the mountains southeast of Jiddah, will give you a good view of the surrounding area. A modern highway bypasses around Mecca, and was especially built for non-Muslim travelers.

Just a little north of Riyadh is Dir'iyah, the ancestral home of the Saud family. Remains of the old fortress-town and its palace can still be seen.

On the east coast, the oasis cities of Qatif and Hofuf are popular places for a day's visit. Thursday market days are especially interesting.

Trips to the islands in the Gulf make good excursions. Tarut Island, now connected by a causeway from Qatif, is said to be the oldest settlement on the Arabian Peninsula. Trips by sailing dhow can be aranged at the al-Khobar and Damman ports.

A weekend trip to Bahrain (an independent island-country) makes a nice change. It can be reached in 15 minutes by air from the Dhahran International Airport, or by dhow.

Especially For Women

There are a number of women's clubs, in Jiddah and Riyadh especially, which emphasize orientation and welcome to new arrivals. They are international, for the most part, and offer opportunities to meet Saudi women as well as those from other guest nations.

In Jiddah, get in touch with the American Ladies of Jiddah. Call the U.S. Embassy for a contact name and telephone number. They publish a useful handbook, covering everything you need to know about establishing a household there, and they hold monthly meetings as well as Newcomers' Teas.

Their organization is limited to Americans; but a similar one, the International Ladies Group, is open to the foreign community. Both offer lectures, art talks, and the like. This group also operates in Riyadh.

Then there are several educational and social centers for both Saudi and foreign women. These offer classes and social events of various kinds and also provide volunteer opportunities.

As one American wife put it:

Tell them when they get there to join one or more of the clubs—to keep their mouths closed but eyes and ears open for the first several weeks—not to jump into anything too fast, but when they are ready, to volunteer their services in whatever appeals to them. Everything else will follow.

As for the Saudi women, never underestimate them. They may not appear much in public, but they have much power to influence the men and they are bright. Don't push or preach or look down on them. Accept their ancient and lovely culture as it is. If they want to change any part of it, they will—in their own time and in their own way. They don't need outsiders telling them anything. Westerners tend to be terribly condescending and that is a real mistake.

In short, my advice is: be quiet, relax, enjoy, get into the flow. It is very different, but it is a wonderful culture, wonderful people, and a great experience to be there.

Especially For Children

Organized groups include Little League baseball, swimming teams sponsored by companies and embassies, Girl and Boy Scouts. And in Riyadh there's a special pony club for children.

The schools also have many recreational facilities. The two schools in Jiddah generally used by Western students are:

- The Parents Cooperative School (PCS), with American curriculum and staff for kindergarten through the 9th grade.
- The Jiddah Preparatory School, operated by the British Embassy and offering the British curriculum for children aged four through ten.

The Riyadh International Community (RICS) School is the only American school in Riyadh, with nursery, kindergarten and grades 1-8. Western children in the Dhahran area attend the

Dhahran Academy, now called The Saudi Arabian International School (SAIS) on the grounds of the U.S. Consulate General compound.

There are several privately owned pre-schools and playgroups in each area and many firms operate schools in remote area compounds.

It is important, however, to take along plenty of toys, games and hobby materials for children. They will probably spend a lot of their playtime at home.

On "Communicating"

As Arabic is the language of the Koran, all Arabs consider it sacred. The Saudi Arabian dialect is nearest of all to the classical and is widely understood throughout the Arab world. Arabs love the sound of their language. They enjoy the complexities of its grammar and its flexibility as a transmitter of thought.

It is a difficult language for Westerners to master, partly because of its complexity and partly because a number of its consonants are made far back in the mouth or throat. These sounds come with practice for most people. But however badly you may do, the Saudis love to have you try to speak their language.

You *can* survive with English alone, especially in Jiddah, Riyadh and the Dhahran area. English is a required subject in Saudi schools from the eighth grade on; most shopkeepers and taxi drivers speak some English; however, a knowledge of Arabic will broaden the scope of your activities and perceptions immeasurably. Mastering even a few words and phrases will make a great deal of difference in your interpersonal relationships. Saudis respond very positively to attempts to speak their lanquage.

There are many opportunities for language study. In the meantime, here are a few hints and some useful phrases to get you started. There is no reason not to start familiarizing yourself with them now.

Pronunciation Key

Transliteration, or translating into English letters from the written Arabic script, varies widely—and you will see different spellings—but the following symbols and sounds should help to keep you on track.

Symbol	Nearest English Sound
a or e	Varying quality, but always short—as in *a*ny, sof*a*, *a*t, b*e*t
ay	As in p*ay*, but sometimes comes out like *i* in b*i*te
i	As in k*i*t
iy or ee	As in mach*i*ne, b*ee*t, h*ea*t
o or ow	As in s*o*, bl*ow*, b*oa*t
aw	As in m*ou*se
u	As in p*u*t
uw or oo	As in b*oo*t

Consonants are the same as in English, with these exceptions:

g	Always hard, as in *g*ood
kh	As in the German "ich" or Scots "loch" (As an approximation, say *aaa*h then move the base of your tongue toward your throat and tense the muscles.)
H	The sound of a labored breath, or an English *h* with extra force
T S D	These "emphatic consonants" do not occur in English. Place your tongue in position for *t*, *s* and *d*, then raise the rear portion toward the roof of your mouth. This produces a heavy sound often only detectable in the vowel that follows.

Doubled vowels and consonants are given double value; that is held twice as long. Called the 'ayn, it is an *ah* sound with the back of the throat constricted as described above.[2]

---

[2] *The Green Book: Guide For Living in Saudi Arabia.* (1980), Pendleton, Madge. Washington, D.C.: Middle East Editorial Associates, p. 105. Used with permission.

Numbers (Important for understanding prices, taxi fares, etc.)

1.	١	waaHid	16.	١٦	sitta'sh
2.	٢	ithnayn	17.	١٧	saba'ta'sh
3.	٣	thalaatha	18.	١٨	thamaanta'sh
4.	٤	arba'a	19.	١٩	tisa'ta'sh
5.	٥	khamsa	20.	٢٠	'ishriyn
6.	٦	sitta	21.	٢١	waaHid wa 'ishriyn
7.	٧	saba'a	22.	٢٢	ithnayn wa 'ishriyn
8.	٨	thamaanya	30.	٣٠	thalathiyn
9.	٩	tisa'a	40.	٤٠	arba'iyn
10.	١٠	'ashara	50.	٥٠	khamsiyn
11.	١١	iHda'sh	60.	٦٠	sittiyn
12.	١٢	ithna'sh	70.	٧٠	saba'iyn
13.	١٣	thalaatta'sh	80.	٨٠	thamaaniyn
14.	١٤	arba'ata'sh	90.	٩٠	tis'iyn
15.	١٥	khamsta'sh	100.	١٠٠	miya

Greetings

Hello (formal)	il salaam 'alaykum	
Hello (response)	wa'alaykum al salaam	
	"Peace be upon you" and "And upon you peace."	
How are you? (to a man)	kayf Haalak?	
How are you? (to a woman)	kayf Haalik?	
	"How is your health?"	
Fine, thanks, and you?	Tayyib, il-Hamdu lillaah, wa unta?	
	"Fine, praise be to God, and you"?	
Good morning	sabaaH il-khayr	
Good morning (response)	sabaaH in-nuwr	"morning of light"
Good afternoon/evening	masa il-khayr-masse'	
Good evening (response)	masa in-nuwr-masse'	"evening of light"
Welcome!	ahlan wa sahlan	Or, "Glad to see you!"
Goodbye	fiy amaan allaah	"Goodbye in the care of God."
Goodbye (response)	fiy amaan il-Kariym	"In the care of God."

Other Useful Words and Phrases

Please	min faDlak (masculine)
Please	min faDlik (feminine)
Thank you	shukran

You're welcome "Don't mention it."	afwan
Sorry, excuse me	muta assif
Never mind "It doesn't matter."	ma'alaysh
Very well, fine, okay	Tayyib
Yes / No	na'am /laa
What	aysh
When	mata (or mita)
Why	laysh
How	kam
Who	miyn
My name is	ismi
What is your name?	aysh ismak? (to a man)
What is your name?	aysh ismik? (to a woman)
I want	ana abgha
How much is how many	kam
Coffee/ Tea	qaHwa / shaay
Do you have	'andak
Where is	fayn(wayn)
Post office	albariyd
Go straight ahead	ruwH ala tuwl
To the right	ala al-yamin
To the left	ala ash-shomaal
How much to the market?	kam ila al suwk?
Ten riyals	'ashara riyaal
No, thanks	laa shukran
Take me to	Waddiniy
Airport	al-matar
Hospital	mustashfah
Today/Tomorrow	alyom/bukrah
Slowly	ala mahlak

To help you get around when you first arrive, here are the Arabic pronunciations for some of the streets and places in Jiddah. (Note, again, that names will not always be spelled the same every time you see them written in the English alphabet.)

The U.S Embassy	as safarah al amarikiyah
The Lebanese Hospital	al mustashfa al libnani
The market (suq)	al suwk
Palestine Square	midan falastin
The Sharafiyah District	sharafiyah
The Bagdadeyah District	bughdadiyah
King Abdul Aziz Road (street)	sharie almalik
Khalid Bin Walid Road (street)	sharie khalid ibn alwalid
The Airport Road (street)	sharie al matar
Medina Road	tariyg al madinah

7

Saudi Arabia: Some Basic Facts

It takes a little time for foreigners to understand the complexities of the Arab cultural heritage, steeped as it is in a long history. Unless and until you begin to appreciate the fundamental place of religion in Saudi Arabian society, for instance, you will never understand much of what goes on around you. Adapting successfully to a new culture calls for some of this understanding and appreciation—not just a list of do's and don'ts.

It is important, therefore, for a newcomer to this land to learn something about its physical environment, its history, its religion, its customs, the Royal House of Al-Saud, and something of its plans for the future, in order to understand why life in Saudi Arabia is like it is.

Besides giving you a basis for understanding attitudes and lifestyles, such information also provides conversational currency—those bits of information that can be "traded" back and forth during informal conversation. This kind of currency can often pave the way for what otherwise might be a rocky road. Saudis will be delighted to know that you are interested enough in them to have learned something about them. In return they will undoubtedly pepper you with questions about the United States.

On the following pages you will find a summary of some facts you will find valuable to know. To pursue any of these subjects further, refer to the reading and resources lists on page 109.

MAP OF SAUDI ARABIA

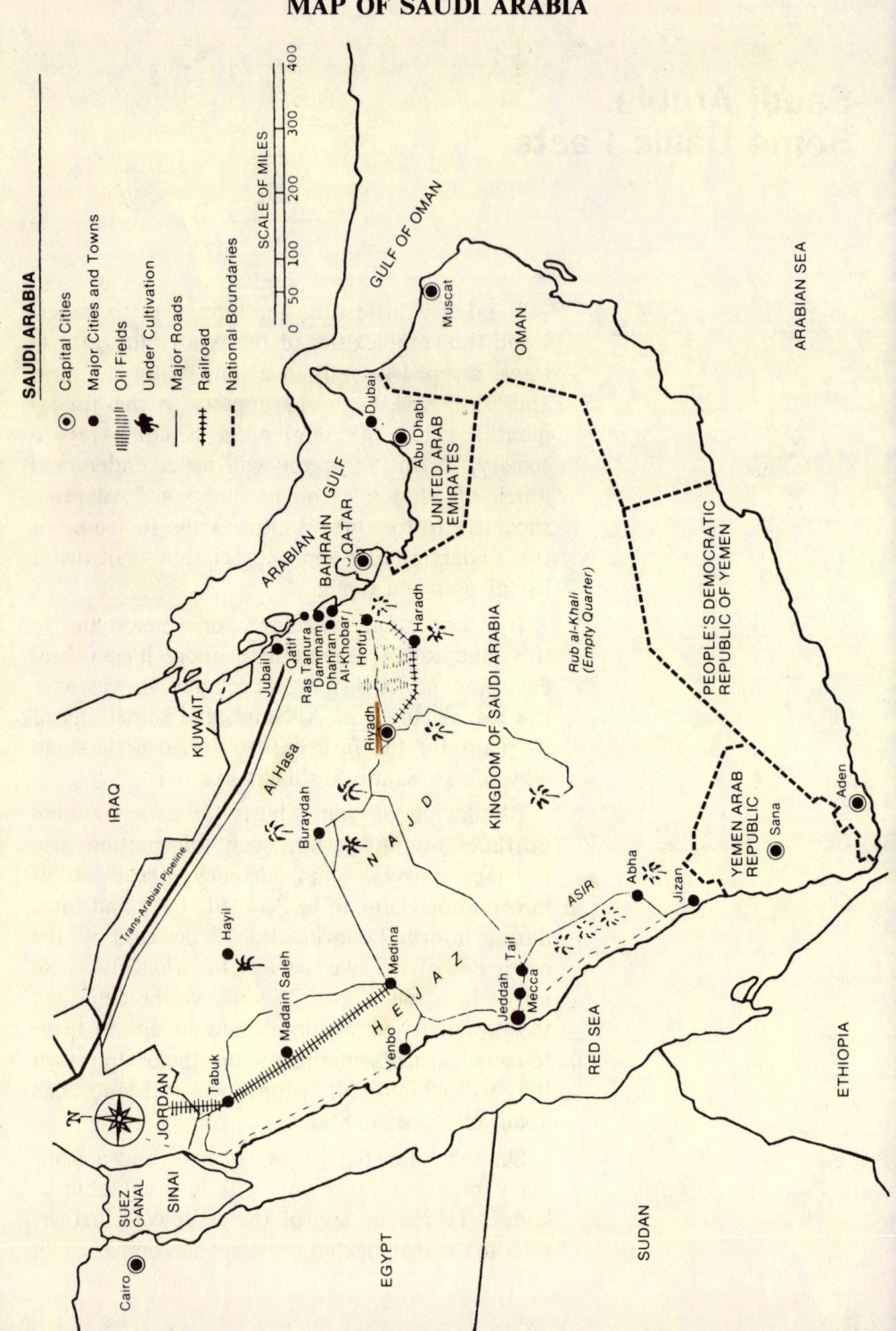

Geography

The Kingdom of Saudi Arabia, with more than 900,000 square miles, occupies four-fifths of the Arabian Peninsula.

The Peninsula, bounded on the north by the deserts of Jordan and Iraq, is surrounded by the sea on the other three sides: the Arabian Sea (Indian Ocean on the south; the Arabian Gulf and Gulf of Oman on the east; and the Red Sea on the west.

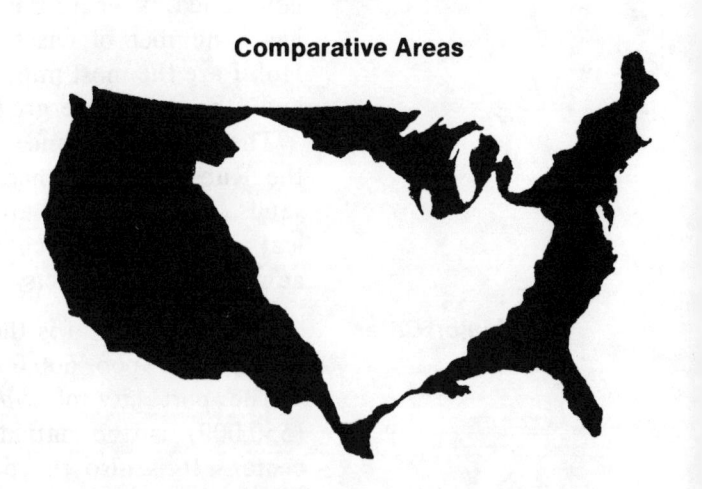

Comparative Areas

Regions

There are four major geographical regions of the country:

The ASIR is the relatively fertile strip of coastal mountains in the extreme southwest (next to Yemen) with peaks up to 10,000 ft. It has sufficient rainfall to permit terraced farming.

The HIJAZ encompasses the balance of the west coast with the mountain chain decreasing somewhat in height as it moves northward, as the coastal plain bordering the Red Sea widens slightly. Here is located the busy port of Jiddah, the country's major business center. Here also are the holiest cities of Islam, Mecca and Medina, which receive more than a million Muslim pilgrims each year.

The NAJD is the vast, eroded plateau in the heart of the Peninsula. At its center is Riyadh, the fast-growing capital. Al-Riyadh means "the gardens" in Arabic, and the city is well planted with greenery, thanks to its springs and ample supply of well water. For the most part, NAJD is arid, although there are some oases in the north. Rub-al Khali, or Empty Quarter, the largest continuous sand desert in the world is located here.

AL HASA, or the Eastern Province as it is now called, is where the oil and gas are. It also has a number of oases, of which Haradh and Hofuf are the most important, where date palms and other crops are grown.

The Eastern Province also includes portions of the Rub al-Khali, where it meets the Jahurah sands. These regions are essentially topographical and do not represent the modern structure of administrative districts.

Major Cities

The royal capital is the modern desert city of *Riyadh* (est. pop. 600,000).

The port city of *Jiddah* on the Red Sea (550,000) is the nation's leading commercial center. It is also the diplomatic capital. The Ministry of Foreign Affairs is here, rather than in Riyadh where all the other ministries are located. More than fifty embassies and a large representation of international commercial and industrial organizations give it the largest foreign population in the Kingdom. A plan is being developed, however, eventually to move the Ministry of Foreign Affairs and the foreign embassy contingent to Riyadh. Most of the Muslim pilgrims bound for *Mecca*, less than 50 miles inland, arrive first in Jiddah. Inland and to the north is *Medina* which shares in the pilgrimage traffic and is growing in importance as a trading center. It is served by a new port at *Yanbu*.

High in the mountains above Mecca is *Taif* the summer capital. To the southwest, in the mountains of the ASIR, is *Abha* and down the coast *Jizan*—both the focus of important agricultural settlements.

On the east coast the two leading commercial centers are *al-Khubar* and the nearby port of *Dammam.* The latter is the Arabian Gulf terminus of the 355-mile rail line to Riyadh.

Close by are the two key oil cities: *Dhahran,* Aramco's American-style home town, and *Ras Tannurah,* the world's largest oil port.

Up the coast, about 50 miles to the north, a new industrial city and port and a naval base are under development at *Jubayl.*

And inland, astride the railroad to Riyadh, are two large oasis-based agricultural centers—*Hofuf* and *Haradh.*

Calendar   Saudi Arabia uses the Islamic calendar initiated more than 1300 years ago. It is based on the *lunar* year rather than the solar year of the Gregorian calendar we use.

Dates are reckoned from the year (622 A.D.) of the Prophet Muhammad's *hijrah* or flight from Mecca to Medina. The Western method of designating Islamic dates is A.H. (Anno Hijrah).

Although containing twelve months, the lunar year is 10-11 days shorter than the solar year. A lunar month is the time between two successive new moons—hence the seasons gradually shift.

The Islamic system follows the ancient convention by which each day begins at sunset. Thus the night precedes the day. What Westerners call Sunday night, Muslims refer to as Monday night (better translated as the eve of Monday). Similar usage is evident in such English phrases as Christmas Eve and New Year's Eve.

Recently the country has officially adopted the international system of reckoning time. Official local time is GMT + 3 hours.

Population

The current population is estimated to be six to eight million. Over half the population is urban. About a quarter are farmers clustered around the small oases. The rest, many hardy Bedouins, are nomads who still lead their flocks of sheep, goats and camels across the arid land in search of pastures.

Climate

In general, it is very hot and very dry—although there are humid coastal regions and some temperate mountain locales. During the long summer months, midday temperatures may soar to over 120°F, though other seasons can be quite pleasant. Temperatures drop dramatically at night in the desert as the heat escapes into a cloudless sky. Winter temperatures in central and northern areas may drop to below freezing.

There are no lakes or permanent streams, and some areas go without rain for years. Average precipitation ranges from 3" annually to as much as 20" in the mountains of the southwest.

History and Government

Americans are inclined to regard the discovery of the New World in 1492 as a long time ago and the birth of Christ as occurring in ancient times. By contrast, the Middle East measures its history in thousands of years, rather than hundreds. Christ was born into a civilization whose history was then at least twice as long as the period since His birth. When Moses lived in Egypt, the Pyramids already were monuments of antiquity.

The recorded history of the Middle East is filled with drama. It is a panorama of the rise and fall of empires. Then came an invigorating force from the Arabian Desert—Islam.

The Arab Empire

Europe was in the Dark Ages when the Prophet Muhammad was born in Mecca in 570 A.D. The Roman Empire had been overrun by barbarians, and to the east the Byzantine Empire lay exhausted from its long struggle against the Persians. The message of Islam proclaimed by Muhammad was so powerful that within a few decades after his death in 632 Arabia had become the fountainhead of a huge new empire, born not so much from a desire for territorial conquest as from a zeal to spread the faith.

Muhammad's spiritual and temporal successors carried on at Medina for a time. Under the Omayyad Dynasty, Damascus became the capital as the power of Islam was stretched all the way across North Africa to Spain and across the Middle East to India.

The Golden Age of the Arab Empire was under the Abbasids (750-1258 A.D.) who maintained their capital in Baghdad. With peace and prosperity came a great flowering of knowledge and the arts. Literature and poetry flourished. The Arabs invented algebra and revolutionized mathematics by introducing the cipher and the floating decimal.

Although the political unity of the Arab Empire soon began to crumble, Islam continued to gain adherents. In Arabia itself, Islam was strengthened by the teachings of an 18th-century reformer, Muhammad ibn abd al-Wahhah, under the patronage of the House of Saud.

Saudi Arabia

The story of Saudi Arabia parallels the history of the House of Saud and its efforts over seven generations to create a unified state. The chronology is complex and the setbacks were many. But the climactic chapter began in 1902 with the daring recapture of Riyadh, the traditional family seat, by a small band whose leader was 21-year-old AbdulAziz ibn Abd ar-Rahman, called ibn-Saud. The next ten years were spent wresting control of the NAJD from the rival Rashid family. Soon after, ibn-Saud regained the Al-Hasa (Eastern Province) from its Turkish occupiers. The southern highlands of ASIR were added to his territory in 1921; Mecca and the HIJAZ were taken in 1925; and in 1927 AbdulAziz was proclaimed king over the entire region.

In 1932 the new nation's name officially became **THE KINGDOM OF SAUDI ARABIA**.

World War I

Midway during this period, World War I caused a number of setbacks.

Long before the discovery of oil, the Middle East was of vital strategic importance—as the geographical link between East and West, the crossroads of commerce between Europe and the Orient. International rivalry for mastery of the area was among the causes of World War I.

The war years were trying for King AbdulAziz. He cooperated with the British when he was not distracted by internal troubles, but the rewards were small. At the end of the war he found himself threatened by an ambitious antagonist, the Sharif Husayn of Mecca in the HIJAZ, who had been armed and supported by the British. (It was Husayn with whom T.E Lawrence rode during the revolt against the Turks in 1916.)

Establishing his royal court in Riyadh, King AbdulAziz worked unstintingly to control the still feuding Bedouin tribes. He was determined to maintain order and create a national identity.

While curbing lawlessness with strong measures, the King assisted the tribes through periods of drought, thereby removing a basic incentive for raids upon neighboring tribes. The result was a relatively high degree of security and stability in the Saudi Kingdom. Another method of binding the tribes to the House of Saud was to marry the daughters of a number of the strongest desert chieftains. Consequently, the royal family today has blood ties throughout the Kingdom and is well informed on whatever is happening.

Currently the King of Saudi Arabia rules with the assistance of a Council of Ministers and an elaborate and relatively effective bureaucracy. The role of the Saud family throughout the government is large and important.

Ties with U.S.

King AbdulAziz opened the country to American oil prospecting in 1933, but it was five years before commercial production began. During the early years of World War II oil development came to a standstill and the number of pilgrims from abroad dwindled, seriously weakening the government's financial position. Both Britain and the United States provided lend-lease and other assistance, and in 1945 Saudi Arabia sided with the Allies in the war.

American and Saudi Arabian Legations were established in the early 1940's, and both missions were raised to embassies in 1949. An historic meeting between President Roosevelt and King AbdulAziz took place on an American cruiser in the Suez Canal in 1945.

Prince Faisal first visited the U.S. in 1943, returning many times as head of his country's delegation to the United Nations, of which Saudi Arabia is a charter member. In 1962, as Crown Prince, he met with President Kennedy. In 1966, on a state visit as King, he held talks with President Johnson.

King AbdulAziz shaped modern Saudi Arabia by cooperating with the West and by encouraging progress in economic and technological fields. He died in 1953 at the age of 73.

He was succeeded by Saud, his eldest son, while Faisal became the Crown Prince. But young Saud's tastes were extravagant and his health poor. In 1964, Faisal was persuaded by the Royal Family to replace his elder brother as King.

King Faisal 1964

King Faisal maintained his father's policy of supporting Muslim orthodoxy. Thus, Saudi Arabia's strict adherence to Islamic tradition continued side by side with the country's economic and administrative development—aimed at building an efficient, modern system of government.

The *Shariah*, the Islamic law which governs questions of human relations and conduct and which is based on the Koran, is officially the country's constitution. Basic rights as well as codes of behavior are integral parts of it.

Interpretation of the *Shariah* is a function of the judiciary (essentially a college of learned religious men) which is independent of the other parts of the government. In matters not expressly stated in this law, authority to enact regulations rests with the King acting through his Council of Ministers.

Under Faisal's guidance, the Saudi economy was stabilized and oil revenues were used to initiate a massive national development program.

Although Saudi Arabia has no national elections or a popularly elected legislature, Faisal continued the tradition of giving all citizens the right of direct petition to the King. Once a week he held open court and any of his subjects could approach him to seek redress of grievances.

It was during such an audience, on March 25, 1975, that Faisal's nephew, bending to kiss the King, drew out a gun and killed him. The assassin prince was beheaded in June with a gold-handled sword as thousands in Riyadh watched. A third brother, Crown Prince Khalid, became King.

King Khalid 1975

King Khalid was born in 1914 and was educated in Riyadh where he received special instruction in Islamic studies from a number of eminent scholars. He had served as Crown Prince since 1964 and had dealt with many domestic and foreign problems relating to the kingdom.

Crown Prince Fahd 1975

On Khalid's succession, Fahd was named the new Crown Prince and appointed Deputy Prime Minister. He chairs a number of councils and committees and functions as King Khalid's right-hand man. In this role, Prince Fahd's enthusiasm for industrialization has contributed to the economic development of the Kingdom.

Religion

Islam is the religious faith of more than 700 million people. It has much in common with Christianity and Judaism, which also originated in the Middle East. (The Arabs regard Abraham as their patriarch.) But the forms differ markedly.

A follower of Islam, a religion of total submission to the will of God, is called a *Muslim*. According to Muslims, elements of their religion were revealed through a long line of prophets, but the full and final revelation was given to *Muhammad* and later embodied in written form in the *Koran*.

The Saudi Arabs are guardians of Islam's two holy cities, *Mecca* (where the Prophet Muhammad was born) and *Medina* (where he died.)

Islam pervades the life of the community of its faithful. Thus, in Saudi Arabia religious law prevails in numerous matters which in other countries fall within the province of civil law.

Although religious law, as embodied in the *Shariah,* has been elaborately developed, the Islamic religion itself is extremely simple and personal.

There are no priests or ministers or congregations like those in Christian churches. The religious concept is one of direct relationship between the individual and God, although joining with others in worship or the pilgrimage to Mecca is deemed meritorious.

Five Pillars of Faith

Five primary duties, known as the five pillars of faith, are required of a Muslim: profession of faith, prayer, almsgiving, fasting and the pilgrimage to Mecca. These are described on page 11.

Muslims believe fervently that theirs is the only true faith. The religion of a good Muslim pervades his whole life. Ordinary conversations contain many references to Allah—because Allah is always present and controls everything.

Indifference to religion, then, is incomprehensible to a Muslim. A show of disrespect for Islam may cause a violent reaction. Muslims spend much time discussing religion, and men who are well versed in and eloquent about it may acquire great influence.

Important Passages From The Koran

Lo! We have sent thee (O Muhammed) with the truth, a bringer of glad tidings.

We have seen the turning of thy face to heaven (for guidance, O Muhammed). And now verily we shall make thee turn (in prayer) toward a place which is dear to thee. So turn thy face toward the Inviolable Place of Worship (Mecca), and ye (O Muslims), wheresoever ye may be, turn your faces (when ye pray) toward it. Allah is not unaware of what ye do.

O ye who believe! When the call is heard (for the prayers of the day) haste unto remembrance of Allah and leave your trading. That is better for you if ye did but know.

* *

O ye who believe! Eat of the good things wherewith we have provided you, and render thanks to Allah. He hath forbidden you only carrion, and blood, and swineflesh, and that which hath been dedicated to (the name of) any other than Allah.

Fasting is prescribed for you that ye may ward off (evil)......and that ye fast is better for you if ye did not know the month of Ramadan in which was revealed the Koran. Whosoever of you is present, let him fast the month, and whosoever of you is sick or on a journey, (let him fast the same) number of other days. Allah desireth for you ease; He desireth not hardship for you.

* *

Allah hath promised those who believe and do good works: Theirs will be forgiveness and immense reward. As for those who believe and do good works, We shall make them enter Gardens (Paradise) underneath which rivers flow-to dwell therein forever; there for them are pure companions—and we shall make them enter plenteous shade.

Language

Arabic—one of the half dozen most widely spoken international languages in use today—is the common tongue of almost 120 million people throughout the Middle East and North Africa. There are three forms:

Classical Arabic is concerned the language of the Koran and a high value is placed on the ability to exploit its riches of vocabulary, grammar and rhyme. While few can really speak even a good imitation of classical Arabic, it remains the standard, or at least the ideal, language. An educated Arab will make frequent use of quotations from the Koran and classical literature in ordinary conversation.

The various dialects, which differ considerably from area to area throughout the Arab world, are used for everyday conversation.

A third form, referred to as *Modern Standard Arabic,* has been developed for written communication and for radio, stage, formal speeches, etc. In grammar, is differs little from classical Arabic; in vocabulary and style, the differences are somewhat more striking.

Arabic is written with a script that has the same ancestry as the Roman alphabet. Its 28 characters may take four different shapes, however, depending on their position in the word. It is written from right to left.

Literature

Arabic is one of the great literary languages of history due to the spread of Islam and the influence of the Holy Koran. The oldest written record in the Arabic language, the Koran, is a work of linguistic eloquence which permanently set the style for classical Arabic. Arabs are known for their love of poetry, which to Western readers often seems narrow and sterile. The explanation of its appeal is found in the melody of the language. To the Arab ear, the sound of Arabic words skillfully used has a sonorous, almost hypnotic effect in which the specific meaning often is secondary. It is this sensual appeal that gives Arabic literature, ancient and modern, its stature among the arts and the poet his high place in Arab society.

Emblems and Symbols

The three most common Saudi symbols, drawn from their religion and cultural heritage, are the *date palm,* the *sword,* and the *Muslim Creed.*

The date palm, which traditionally supplied the main agricultural group, is emblematic of vitality and growth.

The sword, always unsheathed, symbolizes strength rooted in faith. The Muslim Creed "There is no god but God, and Muhammad is the messenger of God," is the first pillar of the Islamic faith.

The national flag, adopted in 1926, bears the creed and the single sword in white on a field of bright green.

Days of the Week

Saturday	as-sabt
Sunday	al-ahad
Monday	al-ithnin
Tuesday	al-Tholatha
Wednesday	al-irb'a
Thursday	al-khamis
Friday	al-jum'a

Months of the Year

Unlike Gregorian months, the months of the Islamic year have no relation to the season and make a complete circuit of the seasons once about every thirty-three Gregorian years. The twelve months of the Islamic year are:

Muharram
Safar
Rabi' al-Awwal
Rabi' al-Thani
Jumad al-Awwal
Jumad al-Thani
Rajab
Sha'ban
Ramadan
Shawwal
Dhu al-Qu'dah
Dhu al-Hijjah

Holidays

Although other Islamic occasions are celebrated by Muslims elsewhere, Saudi Arabia considers only two religious occasions and one secular date as official national holidays.

The most important religious holiday is *Id al-Adha,* the Feast of the Sacrifice, a four-day celebration beginning the tenth day of Dhu al-Hijjah which is the traditional time for the pilgrimage to Mecca.

The second is *Id al-Fitr,* the Feast of the Breaking of the Fast, on the first four days of Shawwal, the month following Ramadan.

National Day commemorates the unification of the country under the new name of the Kingdom of Saudi Arabia. Corresponding more or less to our September 23, it is the only holiday not determined by the Islamic calendar. (It falls on the first day of Libra in the zodiacal calendar.)

THE AMERICAN SAUDI ARABIA RESOURCES

1. About Islam

"The Hajj," by Eve Lee. *The Bridge,* Vol. 5, No. 3, Fall, 1980.

Describes the rites of the Hajj and their significance to Muslims.

"The Hajj: A Special Issue." *ARAMCO World,* Volume 25, Number 6, November-December 1974.

Describes in text and photos the annual pilgrimage to Mecca and Medina.

The Hajj Today, A Survey of the Contemporary Pilgrimage to Mecca, (1979), by David Long. Albany: State Univ. of New York Press.

Long examines not only the religious aspects of the Hajj, but the administrative aspects and the impact of the pilgrimage on Saudi Arabia as the host country.

The Koran Interpreted (1965), by Arthur J. Arberry. New York: MacMillan.

A poetry translation by a well-known British Arab specialist.

The Road to Holy Mecca (1972), by Hussein Hirashina. This Beautiful World Series. New York: Kodansha International. (Distributed by Harper & Row.)

Covers the author's pilgrimage to Mecca, with many photos of Mecca and other parts of Saudi Arabia.

"The Sword and the Sermon," by Thomas J. Abercrombie. *National Geographic,* Vol. 142, No. 1, July 1972, pp. 3-45.

Outlines the history and vastness of the Islamic empire, noting its numerous contributions to Western culture.

2. About Saudi Arabia

Arabia: A Journey Through the Labyrinth (1979), by Jonathan Rabin. New York: Simon and Schuster.

Rabin travels throughout Bahrain, Qatar, Abu Dhabi, Dubai, Yemen, Egypt and

Jordan—letting the people speak for themselves. For some reason he couldn't cut through the red tape to get a visa to visit Saudi Arabia—but the Kingdom is there, through the eyes of its neighbors.

ARAMCO Handbook (1968). New York: Arabian American Oil Company (1345 Avenue of the Americas, New York, N.Y. 10019).
An introduction to Saudi Arabia, its history, geography, government, people and customs, as well as a description of the oil developments in Arabia and the Middle East.

Area Handbook for Saudi Arabia (1977). Washington, D.C.: The American University. (Available through the Superintendent of Documents, U.S. Government Printing Office, Washington, D.C. 20402).

Assignment: Saudi Arabia (1980 rev.). San Francisco: Bechtel Power Corporation.
Useful information on the country and its people and on moving to Saudi Arabia.

At the Drop of Veil (1971) by Marianne Alireza. Boston: Houghton Miffin Company Boston.
The life of a California woman who married a Saudi and spent 13 yrs. in Arabia. Somewhat naive, but good account of one woman's experience.

Businessman's Guide to the Arab World (updated annually). Cambridge: Guides to Multinational Business.
Provides essential business data and the latest economic statistics for 20 countries of the Mideast.

Doing Business in Saudi Arabia (1979), by Nicholas A. Abraham. Boston: Tradeship Publishing.
Covers trade, industrial activity, energy, the customs, laws, business trends and economics, marketing techniques, business style, the do's and dont's of protocol and much more.

Doing Business in Saudi Arabia (latest ed.). New York: Price Waterhouse & Company (1251 Avenue of the Americas, New York, New York, 10020).
Brief practical guide to financial, legal and governmental processes in Saudi Arabia which affect doing business there.

Faisal, King of Saudi Arabia (1966), by Gerald DeGaury. New York: Praeger Publishers.
The first seven chapters are useful resources which deal with the cultural, historical, religious and social setting of Saudi Arabia.

Getting to Know Saudi Arabia (1969), by Ted Phillips. New York: Coward, McCann & Geoghegan, Inc.
Written for children but of interest to adults as well.

Passing Brave (1974), by Wm. R. Polk and Wm. J. Mares. New York: Ballantine Books.
Depicts the passing of the Bedouin way of life.

Saudi Arabia (1976). Washington D.C.: David E. Long Center for Strategic & International Studies, Georgetown University.
Politically oriented study of contemporary Saudi Arabia.

"Saudi Arabia The Kingdom And Its Power," by Robert Azzi. *National Geographic,* Vol. 158, No. 3, September, 1980, pp 286-333.

"The Arab Ethos," by Peter Iseman. *Harpers,* Vol. 256. No. 1533, February, 1978, pp. 37-56.
Excellent article that explores the character, customs and habits of people in Saudi Arabia.

The Green Book: A Guide for Living in Saudi Arabia (1980). by Madge Pendleton, David Davies and Frances Owen Snodgrass. Bethesda: Middle East Editorial Associates. (order from AMIDEAST, 1717 Mass. Avenue N.W., Washington, D.C. 20036).
Provides background and relocation information for faimilies assigned to Saudi Arabia;

written to help newcomers adapt to living there.

The Kingdom of Saudi Arabia (1978). London: Stacey International. (128 Kensington Church Street, London, W8 4BH).

Massive and beautifully done book on all aspects of Saudi Arabia, its history, geography, religion, people and development.

Update: Saudi Arabia (1980), by Alison R. Lanier. Chicago: Intercultural Press, Inc. (70 W. Hubbard St., Chicago, Ill. 60610).

Practical guide for those planning to live in Saudi Arabia. Includes background on history, geography and culture as well as specific information needed by newcomers to the Kingdom.

3. About the Arabic Language

An Introduction to the Arabic Language (n.d.) by Ronald Wolfe. Washington, D.C.: AMIDEAST (1717 Mass. Ave., Washington, D.C. 20036).

A superior brief introduction to the language.

A Practical Guide to Arabic for the Businessman (1978), by Joseph H. Atallah & Nancy A. Shilling. Dallas: Inter-Crescent Publishing Co., Inc. (P.O. Box 8481, Dallas, TX 75205).

A new approach to speaking basic Arabic. Practical Arabic without grammar.

Elemenatry Modern Standard Arabic (1976), by P. F. Abboud *et al.* Ann Arbor: University of Michigan Press.

Second edition of a textbook prepared by a committee of Arabic instructors.

Saudi Arabic: Urban Hijazi Dialect (1975), by Margaret Omar. Washington, D.C.: U.S. State Dept. Foreign Service Institute (available from Superintendent of Documents, Government Printing Office, Washington, D.C. 20402).

Fifteen audio cassette (or reel-to-reel) tapes to accompany this text are available from

National Audio-visual Center, General Services Administration, Order Section, Washington, D.C. 20409.

4. About Learning Languages

Becoming Bilingual: A Guide to Language Learning (1974), by Donald N. Larson and William A. Smalley. Pasadena: William Carey Library (1705 N. Sierra Bonita Ave., Pasadena, CA 91104).

Language Acquisition Made Practical: Field Methods for Language Learning, (1976) by Thomas and Elizabeth Brewster. Colorado Springs: Lingua House (915 W. Jackson, Colorado Springs, CO 80907).

5. About Cross-Cultural Relations

American Cultural Patterns: A Cross-Cultural Perspective (1971), by Edward C. Stewart. Chicago: Intercultural Press, Inc., (70 West Hubbard Street, Chicago, IL 60610).

A penetrating analysis of American ways of thinking and behaving as compared with other cultures.

An Introduction to Inter-Cultural Communication (1975), by John C. Condon and Fathi Yousef. Indianapolis: Bobbs-Merrill.

Provides a basic description of the process of interpersonal communication across cultures with effective use of anecdotes.

The Overseas Americans (1960), by Harland Cleveland, Gerard Mangone and John Adams. New York: McGraw-Hill.

Interesting review of what happened when America responded to its global role after the 2nd World War.

The Silent Language (1963), by Edward T. Hall. Garden City: Doubleday.

Classic study of non-verbal communication in the context of cross-cultural relations.

Survival Kit for Overseas Living (1979), by L. Robert Kohls. Chicago: Intercultural Press, Inc. (70 West Hubbard Street, Chicago, Illinois 60610).

6. Miscellaneous

A lively and practical guide to avoiding culture shock while living abroad.

A Practical Guide to Living and Travel in the Arab World (1978), by Nancy A. Shilling. Dallas: Inter-Crescent Publishing Co., Inc.

Provides essential information for the Western executive handling overseas assignment, personnel evaluation, hiring or orientation involving the Arab World. Includes a major section on Saudi Arabia.

Caravan: The Story of the Middle East (1951), by Carleton S. Coon. New York: Henry Holt & Company.

Lively history.

Desert Gardening, (n.d.). Menlo Park: Lane Publishing Company (Menlo Park, CA, 94025).

Helpful guide for the gardening buff in the desert climate of Saudi Arabia.

Doing Business in Saudi Arabia and the Arab Gulf States (1978-79), by Nancy A. Shilling. Dallas: Inter-Crescent Publishing Co., Inc.

Covers business law, policy and practice in Saudi Arabia and the five Gulf states of Kuwait, Bahrain, Oman, Qatar and the United Arab Emirates.

The Arabs People and Power (1978), prepared by the Editors of the Encyclopedia Britannica. New York: Bantam Books.

General historical perspective on the Arab world. Includes discussions of the political situation in the Middle East and cultural characteristics of the peoples in this area of the world.

The Arab Mind (1973), by Raphael Patai. New York: Charles Scribner's Sons.

Controversial analysis of the way Arabs think and behave. Aimed at the general reader. Commended for its insight by some Arabs, condemned for its exaggeration by others.